THE
STARVED
AND THE
SILENT

THE
STARVED
AND THE
SILENT

ALOYSIUS SCHWARTZ

DOUBLEDAY & COMPANY, INC., GARDEN CITY, NEW YORK, 1966

| *Nihil obstat:* | Gall Higgins, O.F.M. Cap. |
| | *Censor Librorum* |

Imprimatur: ✠	Terence J. Cooke, V.G.
	Archdiocese of New York
	October 26, 1965

The nihil obstat and imprimatur are official declarations that a book or pamphlet is free of doctrinal or moral error. No implication is contained therein that those who have granted the nihil obstat and imprimatur agree with the contents, opinions, or statements expressed.

Library of Congress Catalog Card Number 66–11721
Copyright © 1966 by Aloysius Schwartz
All Rights Reserved
Printed in the United States of America

A la Vièrge
des pauvres.

INTRODUCTION

Still falls the Rain
At the feet of the Starved Man hung upon the cross. . . .
Edith Sitwell, Still Falls the Rain

A victim?
Yet he himself bows to the strokes;
No word comes from him.
Sheep led away to the slaughter-house,
Lamb that stands dumb while it is shorn;
No word from him.
Isaias 53: 7–8

Starved and *Silent:* such is Christ upon the cross. Such, too, is the present condition of the people of Korea.

Christ is the Starved Man, having emptied himself of the last drop of blood and life, having freely given all that he had and surrendered all that he is. He is the Silent Man; as a lamb led to slaughter, he does not open his mouth, nor cry out, nor speak.

The Koreans are one of the many peoples for whom Christ died. They, too, are starved, spiritually and physically. They, too, are silent. Like the poor everywhere and in every time, they lack the power and authority that accompany wealth; therefore, they are unable to cry out and arouse a sleeping world.

The pages which follow are an attempt to speak, in the place of Korea's poor, of what it is like to live in that land today.

In addition to writing of the poor, I have also added personal reflections on the subject of the poverty of Christ. I am aware that Korea has had a proud past and a rich culture; but I have not chosen to write of those things. I have limited myself to two things: the poor of Korea, and the poverty of Christ.

There is a striking similarity between the social-economic structure of Palestine in the time of Christ and that of Korea today. In Palestine, the gap between rich and poor was wide and deep, and virtually unbridgeable. There existed a small number of wealthy people, the landed aristocracy, and most of them lived in Jerusalem; the vast bulk of the population was rural, poverty-stricken, and without prospect of better times. A similar breakdown is to be found in Korea today, where on the one hand you have a group of millionaires whose wealth is constantly increasing, while on the other you have the great masses—lean, hungry, and growing hungrier.

In Christ's Palestine, a drought, an insect plague, or a similar natural disaster usually meant starvation. Unemployment was high, and most of the people were farmers who depended on the soil for their living; their diet was limited to wheat, barley, dried fish, and vegetables. Almost identical conditions prevail in Korea and, by substituting rice for wheat, the diet is almost identical with that of the ancient Palestinians. There are other elements common to both countries: most people own but one change of clothing; often, many families live crowded together in one small house; water is scarce, hygiene is primitive, and medical treatment—at least for the poor—is practically non-existent. Also, in Korea, as in Palestine, there are hundreds of thousands of uncared-for orphan children, beggars, sick, and old people.

The analogy between Palestine *circa* 25 and Korea *circa* 1965 can be carried further than mere generalities; it even applies in individual cases. For example, many of the individuals about whom I write in the first part of this book find their corresponding personalities in the pages of the New Testament. Michael

Rhi, for instance, whom you will meet in Chapter Eight, can be seen as the New Testament character personified by Lazarus in the parable of St. Luke (16:20–31): his portion in this life is bread and ashes; in the next—sweetness and light. And Joseph, who also figures prominently in Part One: he is the sort of person—lost, lonely, hungry—who formed part of the Palestinian multitude on whom Christ took pity. Similarly, the beggars, the children, the farmers, the poor people of Korea today—these, too, easily could have walked out of the pages of the New Testament.

To a great extent, one's surroundings condition one's thinking. Just as day-thinking differs from night-thinking, so does rich-thinking differ from poor-thinking. It is difficult to "think poor" while one is living rich; and it is equally difficult to grasp fully the mind of Christ concerning poverty and the poor while one is living in the lap of luxury. I am not saying that it is impossible; I am saying that it is decidedly difficult.

Christ's amazing doctrine on poverty, and his revolutionary message to the poor, can be understood fully only in the social-economic context in which it was first drawn up and enunciated. Thus, in the first part of this book the reader is introduced to a world of poverty resembling, in many ways, that which Christ knew in his day. The reader, then, will be able to absorb something of the sight, sound, and smell of this world, and vicariously to experience something of the taste and feel of it—not for its own sake, but in order to grasp more clearly the Christian dynamics of poverty and Christ's mind concerning the poor.

In a certain sense, Part One is background music, mental conditioning and remote preparation, for the meditations and reflections which follow in Part Two.

The reader should be warned, however, that *The Starved and the Silent* is not a catechetical treatise of the sort that first poses a question, then follows it immediately with a pat answer. Although the first part of the book indirectly presents the problem of poverty, the second part does not pretend to offer a solution.

Another point I would like to stress in the introduction is that because Christ, the Son of God, freely took upon himself a life of poverty, that state has been permanently sanctified and imbued with a sacramental element. Also, because of Christ's predilection for and his identification with the poor and the disinherited of the earth, these have been given a spiritual quality and anointed for all time with a unique sacred character.

Since the coming of Christ, therefore, it is no longer enough to consider poverty merely from a pragmatic, utilitarian, or humanistic point of view. Christian poverty must be approached existentially, in the sense that it is an inner, religious experience, and, as such, it is a grace involving a certain action of the Spirit. Nor is it enough to treat the poor as would a sociologist, an economist, or a politician. Christian contact with the poor is essentially a contact of faith and charity, or it is nothing.

The inner experience of the dynamics of Christian poverty and the sudden awareness of Christ's presence in the poor can have far-reaching, all-pervading, transformative effects on one's personal life and outlook—much the same as the effects which the incident on the road to Damascus had on the life of Paul of Tarsus. Paul is on his way to Damascus; all of sudden, he is knocked from his horse as by a bolt from the blue. Lying bruised and shaken in the desert sand, he looks up and sees the face of the Risen Christ. Paul is never to be the same again. The vision marks Paul for life and becomes the driving force of his apostolate.

Similarly, a Christian who comes into contact with Christ in the person of the poor and discovers Christ's face in the face of the starved and the silent will be marked and haunted by this vision for life. He can go back to the old dispensation with its long cars, loam carpets, and juicy steaks, but it will no longer be the same. A voice that cannot be stilled will whisper in his ear, saying that it is all folly, that it is all wrong.

In brief, that is something of the spirit in which these pages were written. This book is not intended to be a theological dissertation, an "entertainment," or a work of sociology. It is an experience—an experience which I hope to transmit, however feebly and haltingly, to the reader.

One final item. The events recorded in the first part of the book are based on a diary kept by the author covering a span of approximately seven years. In most instances, names have been changed, and chronology and circumstances altered, in order to protect the identity of certain people and in order to tighten the narrative.

PUSAN, KOREA 1957–1964

PART I

"Blessed are you poor . . ."

CHAPTER ONE

YOU NEVER ASK someone how he got in the French Foreign Legion. It might be embarrassing. By the same token, you should never ask a priest how he got on the foreign missions. It may be personal, and he may be reluctant to tell you.

Nevertheless, the question *is* asked and invariably it follows the same pattern. It goes something like this:

"What diocese are you from, Father?"

"Pusan," I answer.

"Tucson?—Arizona?"

"Pusan—P-u-s-a-n, Korea."

"What are you, a Maryknoller?"

"No."

"Belong to some Order?"

"No, I'm a secular priest of the Pusan diocese."

"Is your bishop Korean?"

"Yes."

"Now, let me get this straight: you are an American secular priest in the Pusan diocese, working under a Korean bishop. Is that right?"

"Yes."

"That's a bit unusual, isn't it? How did that come about?"

The story of a vocation—any vocation—is personal. One is reluctant to talk about it too much, and one is embarrassed by too many probing questions concerning its nature. A vocation is a grace and, like every grace, it should be wrapped and protected in silence. Expose it too much to the open air and it will lose something of its purity, something of its sparkle. Nonetheless, one can speak about a vocation in general terms without being superficial and, at the same time, without sacrificing purity or discretion.

How, then, does a mission vocation begin? Gradually or suddenly? Dramatically or matter-of-factly? In a flash of light, or as the result of years of searching and stumbling?

I do not know about others. I myself grew up with the idea —simply, naturally, and undramatically. From my earliest years in grammar school I can remember wanting nothing else. I remember clearly that I wanted two things: I wanted to be a priest, and I wanted to be a missionary. Later a number three and a number four were added. About the seventh grade in grammar school, I wanted to be a secular priest; and, much later, about the first year in college, I wanted a life of poverty.

In the seventh grade of grammar school I took my first timid steps toward the realization of this vocation in the form of a visit to the local minor seminary, St. Charles' College High School, Catonsville, Maryland. During an interview with the seminary rector, Father George Gleason, a Sulpician, I asked the question: "What if someone wishes to become a missionary priest? Can he come to St. Charles' for four years' high school and then enter the mission society of his choosing?" Father Gleason smiled and asked: "What society are you thinking of?"

"Maryknoll," I said.

He answered: "Yes."

I was thirteen years old when I entered St. Charles'. Our first-year high school class numbered 121 young men, all supposedly desirous of becoming priests. The mortality rate in any seminary is quite high, and St. Charles' proved no exception. So it was that, of this original number of 121, only eleven were ordained.

I liked St. Charles'. It was a good place to begin the long road to the priesthood. It was not, however, a good place to keep alive the spark of a mission vocation. Subsequent experience leads me to generalize in stating that most diocesan seminaries are not excessively preoccupied with fostering mis-

sion vocations in their ranks. Although all the recent popes
have strongly urged bishops to encourage foreign mission vocations in their dioceses, most bishops are too concerned with
their own local needs to make more than token efforts in this
direction. Often, not only do they not encourage vocations to
the field afar, but they actively discourage them. One mission
vocation director whom I know refers contemptuously to this
attitude on the part of certain bishops and seminary superiors
as "spiritual birth control."

St. Charles' College Seminary reflected that parochial attitude. On one occasion, Father Patrick Byrne, a Maryknoll
missionary from Japan who six years later was to die on the
death march into North Korea, paid a visit to the seminary.
The war was just over and Japan, knocked to its knees by defeat and humiliation, was trying to pick itself up by its boot-
straps. Father Byrne was wildly enthusiastic concerning the
possibilities of the Church in postwar Japan and, being a gifted
speaker, his enthusiasm and fervor were contagious. That
night many a young seminarian went to bed dreaming of
faraway places with strange-sounding names and of the possibility of going there themselves. The rector of the seminary
was very upset by Father Byrne's success, and the very next
evening he delivered a counterattack in the form of a long talk
stressing the need for local diocesan vocations. He followed
this up a week later with a visit by a priest from the local
Baltimore Chancery Office. This priest gave a talk similar to
that of the rector; he, too, emphasized the need for local vocations and even hinted that those who sought out other pas-
tures were somehow disloyal to the home diocese. Father
Byrne and the missions didn't have a chance.

Five years later, when I was ready to graduate from high
school at St. Charles', I went to see Father Gleason again. I
asked if he remembered our conversation. Yes, he remembered
it quite well; and, true to his word, he did his best to make my
entrance into Maryknoll smooth and easy when the time came

for me to enroll at Maryknoll Junior College at Lakewood, New Jersey.

Before actually entering the society I had formed in my own mind an image of what I thought "Mister Maryknoll" looked like. As I remember it, I pictured him as something of a cross between Jack Armstrong, the all-American boy, and St. Paul of Tarsus, the Apostle to the Gentiles. The real flesh-and-blood version, which I met for the first time at Lakewood, was of course a bit different.

It can be said of Maryknoll that it is an American institution, founded in America by Americans for Americans—with all the faults and virtues of Americans. For example, in the seminaries, promotion houses, and rest homes of Maryknoll there prevails a genuine hospitality, simplicity, warmth, and joy which I have encountered nowhere else. Within the society itself this atmosphere is deliberately cultivated and is referred to as "the Maryknoll spirit." It is something spontaneous, refreshing, and, in a sense, basically American. At the same time, Maryknoll can boast of, or is afflicted with—depending on one's viewpoint—a highly developed Madison Avenue style, with a typically American flair for publicity and self-advertisement. Maryknoll has succeeded in projecting her image into the minds, hearts—and pocketbooks—of American Catholics as have few other societies. Her extremely smooth, well-oiled publicity and public-relations machine is the envy of many other religious groups and congregations.

Soon after my entry into Maryknoll, however, I became aware of another trait, also typically American, which was to become a source of growing concern for me in the years to follow. In this, Maryknoll was closer to Jack Armstrong and the all-American boy type than to Francis Xavier or Paul of Tarsus. What I discovered was this: Maryknoll was rich; unmistakably so.

In third-year college at Maryknoll, our sociology class tried to determine scientifically the standard of living prevailing in Maryknoll seminaries. After extended discussion, we reached the following conclusion: as regards food, furniture, recreational facilities, general creature comforts and physical ease, the Maryknoll seminarian enjoys a standard of living equivalent to that of the top forty per cent of the American population. The standard of living of the average U.S.-stationed Maryknoll priest is something else again. Having constant access, as he does, to an icebox well stocked with cold beer and soft drinks, a television set, the best of food, and numerous other fringe benefits which are denied the seminarian, the priest enjoys a considerably higher *modus vivendi.*

That situation, of course, is not peculiar to Maryknoll. The standards of Maryknoll are pretty much the standards of most missionary societies in the United States.

The next question is: What of it? After all, isn't this the American way of life? And what is more natural than for an American institution to live in accordance with American standards? If you look at such a standard of living only against an American background, it will hardly appear abnormal. But project it onto a world screen, and the situation changes dramatically. Viewed internationally, the upper forty per cent of the American population becomes the top five per cent of the world population. In other words, the average student at Maryknoll enjoys a standard of living accessible to only five per cent of the people of the world.

Considering that these students are preparing themselves for an apostolate to the poverty-stricken peoples of Asia, Africa, and Latin America, who are at the opposite end of the economic spectrum, one cannot help wondering if this arrangement is not something less than the ideal. That one should prepare for a life among the poor by living rich struck me as being at least a bit illogical. The aforementioned considerations are drawn mostly from the practical order: those of the spiritual order, based on the Gospels and the example of Christ, are infinitely more compelling.

Still, it would be difficult to find fault with those who aspire to a life according to the Gospels—that is, a life of poverty—

while enjoying the "American way of life"—which is to say, a life of comfort and ease—if at the same time two things are present: a certain *malaise* concerning the *status quo*, and a real effort to change it. If one is living well, shall we say, but at the same time inwardly strives toward the ideal of poverty as contained in the Gospels, then the situation is basically a healthy one. If, however, one is living well, never questions the fact, and is devoid of any inner tension toward an ideal of Christian poverty, then the situation leaves something to be desired. My experience indicates that the latter situation prevailed.

For example, a Maryknoll missioner, just back from South America, pays a visit to the seminary and gives a talk to the students. He says: "Sure, we Maryknollers in South America are rich. We don't try to hide the fact. But what of it? We use our riches and our power to benefit the people. In the final analysis, this is all that counts." Another priest, freshly returned from Korea, stops off at the seminary. He, too, gives a talk. He says: "A Maryknoll missioner in the neighboring parish built a new $10,000 rectory. It boasted such luxuries as running water, flush toilets, showers, two refrigerators, large rooms, wide corridors, and spacious veranda. Not much by American standards, perhaps, but by Korean standards it was out of this world—especially considering the fact that it is located in a slum area. After a while the missioner's conscience began to bother him and one day he came to me for advice. I told him, 'Don't worry about it. The people don't expect us to live as they do. Just try to be a little more kind to them and they will forgive you for living rich.'" This type of reasoning of course can be justified. I personally found it unconvincing.

Our Superior at Maryknoll used to remark in his Sunday-evening talks to the seminarians: "The doors swing in and the doors swing out: if you don't like it here you can always look for something else." Which I began to do. I was looking for a society which basically offered three things: the missions, the secular priesthood, and a mystique of Christian poverty. I could not find what I was looking for in the U.S., so I resigned myself to remain with Maryknoll—certainly not the worst fate which could befall a young man aspiring to the mission priesthood.

Then one day the thought occurred to me: Why not try Europe? Maybe there I can find what I'm looking for. So it came about that I discovered the Society of the Auxiliaries of the Missions.

The S.A.M., as the society is known, has its headquarters in Louvain, Belgium. It was founded in 1927 by Father André Boland, a Belgian priest of Walloon (French) descent. Inspired by the ideas of Father Vincent Lebbe, the so-called "Apostle of Modern China," the S.A.M. adopted as its primary goal the training of European secular priests for the dioceses of native-born bishops in Africa and Asia.

Upon reading the life of Father Lebbe I was impressed particularly by one fact: Father Lebbe was a missioner who had an ideal and a mystique of poverty, in many ways resembling that of Francis of Assisi. Father Lebbe, for example, gave this advice to his would-be followers: "The missionary must make every effort and strive constantly toward a goal of effective poverty."

I applied for admission, and after the usual red tape and delay was finally accepted. Some of my friends at Maryknoll were pretty much convinced that I had finally gone off the deep end. But I was starry-eyed and twenty-three, and not to be deterred. So off I went into the wild blue yonder. Only it wasn't blue: it was gray and leaden—the sky of northern Europe such as one finds in Louvain, Belgium.

Did I find what I was looking for at Louvain? Yes—and no. Life at the seminary was poor all right; but it was poor from a poverty born primarily of necessity, not of virtue. We were poor, not so much out of fidelity to a spiritual ideal or mystique as from considerations of a less exalted nature; to wit, we had no money. Still, it was a step in the right direction, and I was more than satisfied with the change.

My five years at Louvain were rewarding ones. I was the only

American at the seminary, the other seminarians being mostly Belgians of Walloon extraction. Contact at an early age with foreign culture and mentality can bring about a psychological release which is a valuable experience and a useful preparation for a future mission apostolate. Theology at the University of Louvain was progressive, and the intellectual atmosphere was open, searching, and liberating.

After ordination to the priesthood I was assigned to Pusan, Korea. As an American priest destined to work in Korea, I could see no advantage in remaining attached to the S.A.M., which is primarily a Belgian society. So in the course of time juridical ties were broken and I became permanently incardinated in Pusan—where I am writing these lines now. This lone-wolf approach to the missions has its obvious advantages and disadvantages. Personally, I like it.

Looking back, however, on my own experience in two mission societies—one in America, one in Europe—and on my own personal experience in Korea, I am convinced that there is need in the Church today for a new mission-sending society. This society should be characterized by three things: 1) international and inter-racial membership, spirit, and formation, 2) secular priesthood, and 3) a mystique of Christian poverty. Of the three, the last is the most important.

CHAPTER TWO

◆

THE ELECTRICITY has gone out. A wind which has come a thousand miles down off the steppes of Russia and the plains of Manchuria howls against the windowpanes causing them to rattle. I can feel its icy breath on the back of my head and neck, and I take the blanket from my shoulders and drape it over my head so that it forms a hood. A single candle burns on the desk before me and its flame flickers and dances to the crazy rhythm of the wind. A wooden crucifix with a gleaming silver corpus protrudes from the bare white wall above the desk and is caught up in the uneven, convulsive play of shadow and light.

I have been in Korea just two days now. What I have seen, heard, and felt during this short time has hit my imagination with all the raw impact of first impression, and I sit here at my desk trying to distill some of these impressions into a few intelligible sentences. But they keep whirring and spinning about like the insides of a slot machine, and all I get is a blur.

I look at the candle and watch as hot tears of wax form slowly at the base of the burning wick, then well up and flow silently down the sides of the stem. The semi-darkness of the room has a soothing effect. Little by little, things stop racing around inside and begin to settle into place.

The day began a little after six at Haneda International Airport in Japan. The Seoul-bound Northwest Airline flight carrying sixty passengers took off on schedule, circled lazily, then pulled away from Tokyo heading northwest for Korea. The sky overhead was a clear, sharp blue, and bright sunlight glinted on the silver wings of the plane. In a short while we were passing the majestic, snow-covered peak of Mount Fuji, its massiveness and splendored loveliness standing out clean against the crystal sky.

We had been aloft a little less than two hours, and a quiet reverie had settled over the cabin of the plane. Now there was a buzz of excitement and a craning of necks.

I looked out and far, far below I could see the blue waters of the Sea of Japan breaking white against the rocky coast of Korea. Then we were passing over range after range of mountains with barren, treeless slopes, small villages with clusters of dun-colored huts with thatched roofs and a patchwork of brown fields, now sown with winter barley. Everything appeared unreal and in slow motion, as if seen through the wrong end of a telescope.

Someone was tugging at my sleeve and I looked up to see the Japanese stewardess motioning to me to fasten my seat belt. At the head of the plane I now saw that the "No Smoking —Fasten Seat Belt" sign had been flashed. I slipped one end of the belt through the other and sat back to wait for the landing. The plane dropped rapidly and the earth was racing beneath us. There was a slight bounce as contact was made, then another; then the engines roared with tremendous power to hold back the plane as it taxied to a stop near the terminal.

I was nearly the last one off the plane. The air tasted clean and fresh after the stuffy atmosphere of the cabin. I trailed a group of people into a small wooden structure which served as a temporary terminal. I filled out some forms rather carelessly and had my visa stamped, then picked up my duffel bag at a counter near the exit door and went outside. The customs official had not even bothered to open my bag and everything was completed in less than five minutes.

Outside there were five or six very old blue Chevrolets which served as taxis, but I could find no bus. I spoke to three of the taxi drivers. The third understood English and I told him to take me to Seoul. As we were about to leave, another Korean raced over and, throwing a quick smile at me, jumped in the seat beside the driver. The dirt road was pockmarked with small chuckholes and the ride was bumpy and jolting. No current of feeling flowed between driver and machine, and he handled the vehicle as he would have driven a stubborn animal.

We were moving at a fast clip now with a light cloud of dust trailing behind. I noticed two little girls walking in our direction about a quarter of a mile down the road. As the distance between us narrowed, they jumped suddenly in front of the car and, almost in the same movement, stepped deftly back to safety. The driver swerved and braked hard as the car came to a stop on the opposite side of the road. When the dust had settled, we glanced back to see the two children racing down the road, making a happy getaway from the scene of their crime. The driver and his companion looked back at me with timid, questioning smiles; then we all laughed and felt less distant from one another because of the common crisis just experienced.

I asked the driver if he could change some money for me at a bank. A foolish question. The driver stopped at an alley, disappeared with my twenty dollars, and in a little while returned with a large stack of dirty hwan notes wrapped in a piece of newspaper. I counted. Eighteen thousand hwan— 8000 more than the official rate of 500 hwan to the dollar. So, within an hour of my arrival in Korea, I was initiated—albeit, unwittingly—in the workings of the black market.

The driver next took me to the railway station and watched happily as I counted out the 5000 hwan he had asked for. One last favor: Would the driver be good enough to purchase a ticket on the next train to Pusan? No, I don't want first class, I want the cheapest. Third class? If that's the cheapest, yes. But *Sinbunim* does not know third class in a Korean train; he would never survive such a trip—the cold, the dirt, the smell; I could not buy you such a ticket. All right, make it second class. Also send a telegram to this address asking them to meet me at the station in Pusan.

The driver returned with ticket, telegram receipt, and the information that my train wasn't leaving until six in the evening. It was now five minutes to twelve. The driver was still hanging around for his tip, which he was not going to get since he had generously overcharged me for: 1) the ride from the airport, 2) the money changing, 3) the railway ticket, and 4) the telegram.

I picked up my duffel bag and asked the driver if it were safe to check it at the railway depot. Sure, it was safe, if I didn't want it back. What can I do with it then? Here, I will put it in the back of my taxi and meet you at the station just before the train leaves. I looked at him level in the eye, long and slow, without saying anything. Perhaps *Sinbunim* does not trust me? Oh, I trust you all right; but still, I think I will keep the duffel bag with me. It will keep me warm while I walk around the streets of Seoul.

I thanked the driver, shook hands, then walked out of the station to see what Korea looks like.

The downtown district isn't too bad with its abundance of department stores, office buildings, hotels, and tea shops. However, as soon as you turn off the main streets into the back alleys and byways, it becomes oppressively grim.

I passed small shoeshine boys, their boxes slung over their shoulders, shivering in the doorways. They were clad in thin, much-worn, much-patched black cotton trousers and shirts. They all wore thin rubber shoes; some had socks, some didn't; some had only one sock and some had socks which did not match. I noticed two small boys sitting on the steps of a bank with one pair of shoes between them: one boy had a shoe on his right foot and the other boy had the matching shoe on his left foot. They were trying to warm themselves in the sun. Another boy whose eyes were watering was whimpering softly to himself, "*Chupta, chupta*" ("So cold, so cold"). A shallow ditch which ran along the alleyway contained stagnant, raw sewage and as I watched a rat dragged its swollen body along the edge, then disappeared into the slime with a soft plumping sound.

The homes I was passing were mostly one-room shack affairs, thrown together with bits of wood, tar paper, canvas, cardboard, and tin. Then I came to a bridge across a river or canal, or rather a wide excavation which at one time had been a river or canal. Here and there it contained pools of black sludge covered over with thin ice. Along the banks were more lean-to's, hovels, and squatters' huts. I walked in a semi-circle, crossing back over another bridge about a hundred yards farther down, and started back toward the center of town. Turning out of a side street, I came upon a long disorderly line of people waiting in front of a wooden shack; in the background there was a large cluster of tent homes. Everyone standing in line held a container of some sort—a bowl, a dish, or a tin can. In large lettering on the side of the wooden shack was written NCWC FEEDING STATION. The door was ajar and smoke and steam were drifting out.

I was back on the main street now. The sidewalks were crowded with people and the streets were noisy with the unrelenting honking of taxi horns. I noticed a young boy coming toward me with a little girl tied tightly to his back with wide swathes of cloth. The little girl's hair was matted and patches had fallen out; the boy's clothes were ragged and dirty. What caught my attention, however, was the expression on the boy's face—an expression which contained all the unself-conscious, uncomplaining, unquestioning sorrow and grief of the world.

The boy had stopped walking now. He wavered uncertainly for an instant, then lay down slowly on the cold pavement among the feet and legs of the hurrying passersby. The child was still tied to his back. Some people stopped, bent down, and offered the boy ten-hwan notes. He stared indifferently ahead of him with a passive, hurt-animal look and made no motion to accept the money. Then someone tried placing the money into the hands of the little girl. At first she grasped the paper in her clenched fists, then began to amuse herself by throwing the bills on the pavement. After a while an older woman stooped down, grasped the boy firmly by his arm, helped him to his feet, and began to scold him gently for lying down on the cold sidewalk. The boy did not resist, but walked off slowly into the crowd, slightly bent forward under the weight of the little girl and his heavy burden of silent grief. The place where he had lain on the pavement was marked by a cluster of fluttering hwan notes.

I continued on my way until I was hungry. The last food I had taken was some eight hours before when coffee and scrambled eggs had been served on the plane. After a little searching I came upon a food stall in an alley and paid a hundred hwan for a Babe Ruth candy bar. I unwrapped it, bit into it hungrily, and found the taste of the chocolate and nuts so stale and bitter that I spit out the first mouthful and threw the remainder away. A little girl, who had been secretly watching me, raced over, picked up the candy, and began to wolf it down, making me feel rather ashamed.

I turned into the first eating shop I saw and sat down on a rickety wooden bench before a bare wooden table. The interior of the restaurant was small and not too clean, but it was warm and it felt good to be inside, away from the cold. There were only six tables in the shop, two of which were occupied.

As I sat down, the other customers, who had previously been talking quite volubly, suddenly grew very still. They moved their rice-laden chopsticks slowly and deliberately now, casting furtive glances in my direction. The glances were neither hostile nor friendly—just curious. A girl was standing by my table obviously waiting for an order. Just then I would have given much to have been able to speak Korean. I spoke in English and I could see that she did not understand. She hurried away, however, and in a few minutes reappeared with a plate of steaming dumplings, a pair of chopsticks, and a cup of hot rice water. "*Komapsumnida,*" I said, "Thank you." The girl giggled, hiding her mouth with her hand, and the others smiled approvingly.

I could feel the others watching me with much expectancy as I picked up the chopsticks and began eating. I managed to get the food in by using a pushing, shoveling motion—unorthodox, perhaps, but effective nonetheless. The food felt good going down and I could feel its warmth spreading through my insides.

I stayed in the shop an hour, enjoying the strange sounds, smells, and atmosphere. Then I paid my bill and with one hand on the door, ready to leave, I turned and said in a loud voice, *"Annyonghi kyesipsio, komapsumnida"*—"Goodby thanks." These words pretty much exhausted my stock of Korean, but they brought pleasure to my audience, for as I closed the door behind me they were smiling and nodding approvingly.

It had grown dark now and the night sky of Korea was spangled with bright silver stars. As I looked up, I thought of what John Chang had told me of night in Korea one afternoon several years ago as we walked along together through the damp streets of Louvain under a gray, leaden sky. "The sky in my country never grows black," he had said, "it deepens from one shade of blue to another until it reaches a perfect shade and depth of dark blue, then the stars come out and begin to shine. Really, I have seen nothing as beautiful as the night sky of Korea." As he said this, I remember how his eyes grew moist and how the corners of his eyes began to fill with tears. But it was so: night in Korea was beautiful and merciful, as well, hiding as it did the harsh realities of the day.

My train was leaving in a half hour. I hurried over to the railway station and had ample time to get lost and board the wrong train before an understanding conductor, who spoke a little English, guided me to the right train just five minutes before it chugged out of the Seoul Station, heading south-southeast for Taejon, Taegu, and Pusan.

As the train worked up steam and began to hit its stride, I settled back and studied the faces of the people about me. They were tough, stolid, uncomplaining faces that reached back across 4000 years of history into the mountains of Manchuria and the plains of Mongolia. In the lines of the faces one could read the moral fiber of a people whom a half century and more of tragedy had not been able to break. The faces were hard, but they were handsome, with broad forehead, high cheekbones, regular features, and light-brown complexion; the dark eyes were as sad and melancholy as the tender Korean night through which our train was passing.

I had been dozing. I was wakened as the train began braking to a stop with much hissing and jolting. I took the watch from my pocket. Three-thirty. We're in Taegu then.

The wheels of the train were still screeching to a stop when the door to our car swung open and a group of boys swarmed in. They were about ten in number, between the ages of six and twelve.

It was as though someone had emptied a pack of caged rodents into the car. In an instant the boys were racing down the aisles, scurrying under seats, and reaching between the legs of passengers for discarded pop bottles, scraps of food, and cigarette butts. They pushed the food hungrily into their mouths, then washed it down with what remained in the pop bottles. They placed the cigarette butts into cloth bags which hung from their belts, and they placed the pop bottles into burlap sacks which they trailed along the floor. Their movements were quick and furtive. All the while they kept glancing over their shoulders for the first sign of approaching danger in the person of the conductor.

The boys were uniformly filthy and in rags, and their eyes burned with a fierce, scared, hunted-animal expression which betrayed the dog-eat-dog existence they lived. One of the boys' faces had been beaten black and blue; another had a running ulcer just under the nose; another boy's face was grotesquely wrinkled and disfigured like that of an old, old man.

When the conductor appeared in the doorway, the boys scampered out of the car in near-panic, carrying their spoils with them. The whole episode had happened so quickly that it had an unreal and apocalyptic, almost nightmarish quality about it.

As the train began to move again, I pressed my face against the window and looked out into the night. I could make out clearly the rugged form of treeless mountains etched against the blue-black sky.

I got up and went to the washroom. I threw some cold water on my face, combed my hair, then wiped the soot and grime from my clothes. The train was slowing down now and I knew we were coming into Pusan. It was nearly five o'clock. I got my bag down and waited in the aisle behind a shuffling line of impatient people. The train stopped with a slightly spastic movement. When my turn came to step down from the train onto the platform I could feel my heart beating very fast with nervous expectancy.

I looked up and down the platform, then spotted Father Chang racing over to greet me. It was three years since I had said good-by to him at the *Gare* in Louvain; now he was pastor of the Central Church in Pusan. He took my hand in both of his and held it warmly while speaking excitedly in French.

A welcoming delegation of a hundred Catholics was forming about us. When they were in place there was a pause and a little girl stepped forward to present me with a large bouquet of flowers. The people beamed and applauded politely. Father Chang took me by the arm, led me to a waiting jeep, and we sped through dark, totally empty streets, to arrive in a few minutes at the Central Church and the bishop's house.

Father Chang led me to the sacristy where I began vesting for Mass. From the door of the sacristy I could see people filing in and taking their places in the dimly lit church, men on one side, women on the other. They were mostly the same people who had been at the railway station a few minutes before to greet me. At a signal from Father Chang I entered the sanctuary to begin Mass. At the same time I could feel a hundred pairs of eyes burning the side of my face, taking in the difference of complexion, color of hair, and length of nose. I was a stranger in a strange land and, for the first time since my arrival in Korea, I felt it.

After Mass, Father Chang led me across a narrow courtyard to a small, three-story building which served at the same time as the bishop's house, Chancery Office, residence for visiting priests, parish hall, and a few other things. We climbed to the third floor, knocked at the door of the bishop's room, slipped off our shoes, and entered just as the bishop was emerging from his private chapel. Bishop Choi flashed a warm expansive smile as I knelt down to kiss his ring.

The first thing which struck me about Bishop Choi was his youthful, almost boyish appearance. Although in his early fifties, he looks considerably younger. The bishop received me warmly and in his inimitable mixture of kitchen Latin and fractured English expressed his delight at my coming to Pusan. Then he began to speak of his need for priests.

The Diocese of Pusan numbers more than 4,000,000 souls, but Bishop Choi has only fifty priests, foreign and Korean, to work with. Ten years ago there were less than 20,000 Catholics in the area; today the number is close to 95,000. Last year there were 10,000 adult converts and, at present, 5000 catechumens are preparing to enter the Church. As I was leaving his room, Bishop Choi asked me to write to priests in America inviting, urging, begging them to come to Korea where the harvest is great but the laborers are few.

After leaving the bishop's room, I went upstairs to the roof veranda and looked out over the city. My city now.

I thought of the task that lay ahead. The French have a term for it, *adaptation totale*: when in Rome not only do as the Romans do, but also think, speak, react, judge, and feel as they do. Jew with the Jews, Greek with the Greeks, and Korean with the Koreans. But one does not change his nationality as he does a shirt. It is not that easy. The psychological wellspring of the Korean people goes back thousands of years. Their thought is marked by a millenary tradition of Buddhism and Confucianism. Their temperament has been molded by the ageless mountains which are everywhere present, by the unfriendly earth from which they wrest their living, and by the restless waves which lap their shores. Their emotions, feelings, hopes, and desires bear the stamp of past decades of suffering and at present they are being shaped anew by the all-pervading influence of Western materialism, scientism, and hedonism.

The honeymoon, the romance, the glamour of being in a foreign land with its different sights, sounds, and smells lasts but a few weeks or, at most, a few months. Then begins the day-to-day grind of mastering a new language, and the day-in, day-out struggle of accustoming oneself to a new way of living. To become one of them and one with them is the task of a lifetime and, I have been told, it is not child's play.

◆

CHAPTER THREE

◆

Pusan pulsates with life. Its streets teem with people and at night you wonder how they all can possibly fit inside.

There seem to be few dogs, cats, birds, trees, shrubs, or other forms of animal and vegetable life in Pusan. Just people. Thousands of them, everywhere you go; elbowing each other, hurrying past each other, staring at each other, talking, laughing, working, playing, struggling for existence, fighting for a place in the sun.

Fifteen years ago the population of Pusan was 250,000; today it is 1,200,000—and still growing. At first the city was built on a strip of land between the mountains and the bay. Then came the Korean War, and with the war, the refugees—wave upon wave of them. After the armistice, many of the refugees stayed on. Added to this was the steady trickle of people from farm areas making their way to the city in search of food and work. Thousands of one-room shacks and squatter huts sprouted like fungus on the bare mountain slopes surrounding Pusan, and tent cities sprang up almost overnight.

It was two weeks after my arrival before I got a chance to inspect Pusan. The day was raw and cold—hardly suitable for sightseeing; but we—Damiano, my Korean language instructor, and I—went anyhow.

Leaving the bishop's house, we walked swiftly along a few crowded downtown streets, dodging occasionally to avoid being hit by taxis, and stepping aside now and then to miss colliding with children playing hopscotch and jump rope on the sidewalks. In a few minutes we had begun climbing the mountain just opposite the bishop's house, and our breath came hard and short as we picked our way along a steep, slippery path. In some places, large steps had been hacked out of the dirt slope; in others, the footpath which we were following led over a rickety, wooden parapet, with a drop of twenty feet below. At one point in our climb, our path was blocked by a youngster swiveling a hula hoop and we had to wait until he was ready to step aside.

On both sides of the footpath stood the homes of Pusan's "cliff dwellers": tents, lean-to's, hovels, and huts of every size, shape, form, and description. The angles at which some of these dwellings had come to rest seem to defy the laws of physics. Many of them are supported by stilts and others are perched so precariously on the mountain slope that it seems the first strong gust of wind will carry them away.

As we continued along, a small band of children began forming behind us—laughing, shouting, happy kids, enjoying immensely the presence of a *khojaengi* (big-nose) in their midst. The youngsters kept repeating a phrase in a singsong fashion which at first I couldn't get.

At one point I turned about to face them and the children scurried to the four winds amid loud shrieking and laughter. Then they fell in line and once again took up their teasing chant, which I began to make out as "hallokay, hallokay, hallokay." I asked Damiano and, sure enough, that's what it was. He explained, somewhat embarrassedly, that this is what Korean children call Americans: "Hallokays," a contraction made up of "hello" and "okay."

After a while, Damiano turned off onto a side path and I followed him until we came to a low tent-like structure. Damiano pulled back the canvas flap, stuck his head inside, and said something in Korean. Then he took off his mud-caked shoes and stooped low to crawl in. He motioned for me to follow. Inside were four young men between the ages of twenty and thirty. I learned that all of them had TB. They were on the Maryknoll Sisters' TB program, and once a week the Sisters bring them food and medicine.

After leaving the tent which housed the TB patients, Damiano and I continued our climb until we reached a point just below the ridge of the mountain. The air was fresh and clean here—free of the stupefying odors of sweat, excrement, and garbage which hung over the streets below. I watched a jiggey carrier moving slowly under an enormous burden across the crest of the mountain; the deepening light of late afternoon was behind him, creating a perfect silhouette.

I looked over and saw Damiano standing at the doorway of a cave hut, talking to a tall emaciated man with long hair, who was blinking in the strong light. I went over and was introduced to Christopher Lee. Christopher smiled warmly, shook hands, and insisted that we go inside. There were no windows in the dwelling, and the air inside was stale and rank.

Christopher used to be a high school teacher but gave it up because of bad health. Now, he teaches Christian doctrine to the families who live in the huts about and below him, and he also teaches the children how to read and write. Last year he prepared more than a hundred converts for baptism. He receives no salary for this work, and he manages to sustain himself by making homemade bread and selling it in the Pusan market.

After leaving Christopher, we walked along a path leading downward from the mountain until we reached level ground. We came to a stream which cuts through the west side of the city and began following it. The water of the stream was foul and full of filth; its color was grayish, and it flowed sluggishly toward the bay like thin oatmeal.

On both sides of the stream, from the base of the embankment to the water, lay a stretch of dry ground. A number of makeshift shelters had been built in that area. Farther along, we passed some bridges under which a number of families had set up housekeeping. Still later, we came upon a rusting, discarded Ford automobile which, wheelless, rested on blocks near the edge of the water and served as living quarters for someone or some family.

Then we passed a shack built against the stone wall of the embankment, its roof level with the road on which we were walking. Several boys were sitting near the door of the shack, trying to warm themselves in the afternoon sunlight, which was trapped and reflected by the wall behind them. They were talking in low, murmurous tones. Large, empty wicker baskets were lying about in disorder, and a huge pile of damp paper and rags stretched away almost to the water's edge.

I grabbed Damiano by the sleeve and we walked back to a point just above the entrance to the shack. We stood there for a while until one of the boys noticed us. He said something to the others in a low voice and they all looked up at us with a half-hostile, half-curious, what-do-you-want stare.

Damiano asked if they minded if we came down for a visit. They didn't. Since I could find no other way of getting down, I jumped. Damiano followed. One boy held aside the blanket covering the entrance to the shack and we stooped to go in. Inside, four boys were lying on the dirt floor, wrapped in khaki blankets. As we entered, they got up one by one, rubbing the sleep out of their eyes with their fists. Then they came over to join the circle which was forming about Damiano and myself. A few rays of light filtered in through cracks in the wooden walls; otherwise the shelter was completely dark.

Damiano introduced us, exchanged a few pleasantries, then asked the boys to tell us a little about themselves. At first I feared that they would be offended by our intrusion. But as the boys began speaking freely and without restraint, I realized that my fears were groundless. On the contrary, they seemed genuinely pleased by the interest being shown them.

The boys were a group of ragpickers—just one of many such in Pusan. Most of them are between the ages of twenty and thirty and live in small gangs such as this one. It is es-

timated that there are 2000 young men engaged in this pro-
fession in the Pusan area.

The community which we were visiting had eleven members, all of whom lived in a one-room shack about twelve feet
long and six feet wide. At night, they explained, there was
just enough room for each of the eleven to wrap himself in a
blanket and curl up to sleep on the dirt floor. There was no
heat in the cabin, but no one seemed to mind except the two
visitors who were chilled to the bone.

The ragpicker's day begins at dawn. He rises, slips a wicker
basket onto his back, and starts making the rounds of Pusan's
streets and alleys, picking up scraps of paper, cardboard, and
rags. By midday there is not a trash heap in the entire city
which has escaped the ragpickers' prodding tongs. In the afternoon the ragpicker returns home with his day's loot on his
back. He empties the basket and sorts the contents. The
damp paper is spread in the sun to dry; the rags are tied into
bundles. After it is dry, he sells it to a cardboard manufacturer.
On an average day a ragpicker earns about forty hwan (four
cents), which is enough, or almost enough, to purchase one
meal's supply of rice.

In the evening the ragpicker takes his number-ten tin can
and makes the rounds of the restaurants and the homes of the
more well-to-do, begging for supplementary food. Then he returns home to sleep before beginning another day similar to
the one which preceded it.

Sitting there on the dirt floor, I looked up through the dim
light at the circle of faces about me. The faces all indicated
that they had not come into contact with soap and water for
quite some time. In Korea, cleanliness is a luxury which the
very poor cannot afford.

I noticed that one of the boys' faces was smeared with some
kind of red, Mercurochrome-like coloring. I asked what was the
matter. Had he been hurt? This brought a ripple of laughter
from the encircling group. No, he wasn't hurt or anything like

that. He marks himself up just for laughs. He is the joker of the community, the comedian, the self-appointed clown.

Speaking of clowns, there was something of a circus air about the clothes which the boys wore. There were unbelievable assortments and combinations of rags and tattered garments. There was nothing funny about the group, however, nothing which lent itself to laughter. They were forced to lead a hand-to-mouth, dog-eat-dog existence and it showed. It was visible in the expression on their faces and the look in their eyes.

Damiano and I got up to leave, shook hands all around, then walked out into the daylight. The leader of the group escorted us to a makeshift ladder a short distance from the shack. We climbed up, waved good-by to the group assembled below, then headed back toward the bishop's house.

On the way back, Damiano cleared his throat and said somewhat solemnly: "Now, *Sinbunim*, you know what it is like to be poor in Korea."

"*Nae*, "*kurohsumnida*." (Yes, sure.)

◆

CHAPTER FOUR

◆

ONLY IN the villages will you find the true Korea," said Bishop Choi.

And he said it so often that I finally gave in and began making plans for my own personal discovery of the "true" Korea.

I asked Damiano to write his relatives in Nam-sa—a small village eighty miles northeast of Pusan—to inquire if I would be welcome for a short visit. The reply came by return mail. Not only would the "Spiritual Father" be welcome: he would be most welcome. Indeed it would be an unspeakable honor to receive the "Spiritual Father" because never before had a non-Korean sojourned in the humble village of Nam-sa. Damiano was happy to go along as guide and interpreter. It was a bright sunny March afternoon when we boarded the three-thirty local bound for Chinju—the jumping-off point for Nam-sa.

It was dark by the time our slow train had come to a stop in the terminal at Chinju. It cost a dollar to go by jeep-taxi from the railway station to the Catholic Mission on the other side of the city where we planned to spend the night. The houseboy let us in and informed us that the two Franciscan Fathers who lived there were away on mission trips. Then the houseboy prepared a supper of rice, scrambled eggs, and coffee. After supper he showed us to our rooms.

About four o'clock in the morning I was awakened by the reverberations of a gong, so loud that at first I thought it was located at the foot of my bed. A little later the acrid smell of burning incense wafted into the room. It was then I discovered that a Buddhist monastery was immediately adjacent to the

Catholic Mission. After Mass and breakfast, Damiano and I sauntered over to the monastery to see for ourselves what manner of men rise at four in the morning, beat gongs, burn incense, and pray while the rest of the world sleeps. Better: tries to sleep.

We entered the sun-filled courtyard of the monastery just as a group of monks were emerging from a small reading room which opened onto the veranda. The monks were wearing loose-fitting habits made of coarse-fibered, gray cotton cloth. One young monk, seeing Damiano and me standing rather aimlessly in the center of the courtyard, detached himself from the group and came over to us. With hands folded on his breast and eyes lowered, the monk bowed before us slowly and gracefully. He then offered to show us about the monastery and started off immediately in the direction of the temple. We followed close behind.

In front of the temple, mounted on the end of a twenty-foot pole, was a rather startling sight: a swastika. I had always associated this ugly symbol with Hitler's Nazis, and it was something of a shock to stumble upon it in this out-of-the-way corner of the globe. But there it was, boldly outlined against the open blue sky. As I stood gaping up at it, a memory stirred in the corner of my mind of having read somewhere that the swastika was originally a symbol of the Divinity, borrowed from ancient Egyptian sun worshipers and, as such, had nothing to do with Nazism. By what circuitous route the symbol found its way to this monastery, and what it means today standing guard at the entrance to a Buddhist temple, is a problem I gladly leave to the savant.

We removed our shoes and stepped onto the soft, elastic mat flooring of the temple. The absence of all furnishings and accouterments in the interior of the temple gave it an unadorned and ascetical air which impressed me as being very spiritual and religious. Against the wall in the center of the room loomed the massive figure of a golden Buddha. With fat belly, flaccid features, legs crossed, hands folded in his lap, and eyes lowered, there he sat calmly contemplating his bellybutton. His very posture was introspective and self-oriented—as if he wished to become wrapped up in himself. Gray smoke from burning incense curled lazily before the opulent statue and rose slowly to the ceiling.

I looked long at this statue. I could not help contrasting it with the symbol of Christianity: that of a gaunt Figure nailed to a tree in a posture of torture, agony, and defeat; drained of the last drop of blood and water; arms outstretched to embrace the world. Christ is lifted up to the heavens on a cross, while Buddha is weighed down in his own fatness and complacency. The two figures, taken as symbols of living beliefs, could hardly be more dramatically opposed.

Upon leaving the temple, I asked the young monk who was acting as guide to explain why he himself had embraced the monastic life. He hesitated a moment to collect his thoughts, then, eyes downcast, began speaking in a soft, low voice.

"The name Buddha means 'I am awake' and, while the rest of the world dozed, Buddha pierced to the heart of the mystery of life. It came about in this manner. In India around 560 B.C. there was born of wealthy and noble parents a son, named Gautama, destined to become Buddha, The Enlightened One. As a youth and a young man, Buddha's parents hid from him the sight of the harsher realities of life. One day on a fateful journey which was to transform his life, Buddha successively encountered an old man, a sick man, a dead man, and a holy man. For the first time Buddha discovered the facts of old age, sickness, death, and the possibility of withdrawing from the world. From this experience he perceived that worldly existence is vanity, and so he decided to withdraw from the world. He left his palace, his riches, his model wife, and his lovely son, and embarked on a life of asceticism and meditation."

Speaking even more softly than before, the young monk continued:

"I have read the life of Buddha many times and I have also read the lives of many Buddhist saints. Little by little, I myself have come to realize that life in society is vain and that all existence is empty. In the monastery, through prayer, pious reading, and asceticism, one learns to dominate emotions, desires, and passions; if successful, a monk will arrive eventually at the state of total apathy, or inner nothingness, called *Nirvana*.

"In this state of inner enlightenment, one experiences neither pain nor pleasure, and this is the highest happiness. To the Buddhist, life is simple, and happiness consists merely in not being unhappy. In many Buddhist monasteries, for example, we recite a litany which reveals our inmost philosophy. Eyes closed, sitting on the floor, swaying gently back and forth, we sing and chant together: 'Ninety-nine desires, ninety-nine sorrows. Ninety-eight desires, ninety-eight sorrows. Ninety-seven desires, ninety-seven sorrows.' And so on, until—'No desires, no sorrows!' To attain that, I have entered this monastery."

Patiently, the monk answered a few more of my questions: in this monastery there were fifteen monks; they were mostly young, they were all celibate, they depended on alms for their sustenance.

I thanked our kind host and came away from the tour with the impression that, although Buddhist monasteries in Korea certainly contain their share of charlatans and leeches, they also have a number of authentic mystics and holy men.

On the way back to the mission Damiano told me that, several years ago, the Buddhist monks in Korea had split into two openly opposed factions—one for and one against the right of monks to marry. It was a rather ugly, knock-down, drag-out battle in which both sides resorted to physical violence. When the controversy finally ended, Buddhism in Korea had suffered another heavy blow to its ever-diminishing prestige and vitality.

It was nine-thirty when we returned to the Mission. We picked up our bags and started off in the direction of the bus station. As we walked down the path leading away from the Mission, a high-bouncing, fast-moving jeep came toward us out of a cloud of dust. It was Father Giupponi.

Father braked hard, and as he alighted from the jeep he smiled warmly and extended his hand. Father Giupponi, age forty-three, native of Italy, Franciscan priest, came to Korea five years ago after being expelled from China by the Communists. In a slender frame he embodies all the warmth and gentleness of the Latins and one is always at ease in his company. Father Giupponi ordered us into his jeep and told us that, after he had had a chance to wash his face and drink a cup of coffee, he would drive us to our destination.

The ride over the bumpy, dusty, deeply pocked and scarred roads to Nam-sa was a kidney-breaking experience. The tough little jeep and its veteran driver did not seem to mind, but Damiano and I were rattled to the teeth.

The terrain was mountainous and the road was winding. We passed village after village, each one a copy of the one before. Then we came to a wide shallow river sparkling in the sunlight and crossed over a bridge into a village on the other side. Damiano cleared his throat in preparation for an announcement, then happily declared that we had arrived. This was it—Nam-sa.

Stepping down from the jeep, we breathed in the pure, fresh, mountain air, and at the same time looked about at the surrounding countryside.

The change from Pusan was striking. Instead of ugly tents and squatter huts which crowded every square inch of space as in Pusan, here could be seen only picturesque thatched-roof huts and cottages, poor no doubt, but still not lacking in dignity. The dirty smokestacks and chimneys of the city were now replaced by open fields green with winter barley and by the beautiful contour of hills and mountains rising in the background. Instead of the incessant honking of taxi horns, as in Pusan, here could be heard only the soft music of the gently flowing river which cuts through the village. The fields were dotted with farmers in traditional white garb, sprinkling fertilizer, weeding, and turning over the soil in preparation for the planting of rice. Seen beneath an unclouded azure sky, the scene stretching away before us was almost idyllic.

One had to remind himself, however, that the idyllic element in the lives of these people is on the surface. Actually, the struggle for survival in Korea's villages is more difficult than in its cities. In the cities—thanks in part to American relief matériel—there is usually something to eat, even though it may be only a bowl of cornmeal mush. This is not always the case in the villages, where each spring brings with it the specter of hunger and where hunger occasionally turns into starvation. Seventy per cent of the people in South Korea live off the land. Or, to be more precise: *try* to live off the land. With mountains everywhere and taking up all the room, less than twenty per cent of the land is arable. Much of the wealth has been drained from the soil by overintensive cultivation and insufficient fertilization. The brown earth of Korea is now tired and hungry; crops produced from it do not have the same food value as those produced in the richer soil of Western countries. Those who try to wrest their living from the earth of this rugged peninsula have a hard time of it indeed.

Time was in Korea when the land was sweet and good and would keep in modest contentment those who tried to live from it. Life in those days was far from easy, but it was livable. The population was stable, and village economy was independent and self-sufficient. Then came the Japanese, and with them came industry, modern medicine, hygiene—in a word, Progress.

The Japanese introduced small factories which produced consumer goods and village economy was shattered, completely and forevermore. For example, instead of the sandals which village artisans formerly fashioned from hemp, merchants now brought in factory-made rubber shoes from the cities. Instead of homemade earthenware jugs for carrying water, tin pails manufactured in the cities were now sold and bought in the villages. And so on. Finally, the formerly independent farmer found himself totally dependent upon the city, and he was often forced to go into debt to buy things which his father and grandfather, and his father before him, had produced themselves from their own resources.

The first impact of modern medicine and hygiene in an underdeveloped country always results in a phenomenal reduction of the mortality rate. Korea is no exception. In 1920, the population of Korea was less than 20,000,000; today it is 38,000,000, and it is still growing at the astounding rate of three per cent a year. The land cannot support such a multitude and there is not sufficient industry in the cities to absorb the resulting rural overflow. As a matter of fact, *per capita* farm output in Korea has fallen ten per cent below its prewar level.

All this, of course, is Progress. Its coming is inevitable, but one cannot but wonder: must it always act like a bull in a china shop? In less than a decade, Progress has left in shambles a delicate balance which nature took a thousand generations to work out.

My reflections on the plight of the Korean farmer were interrupted by Father Giupponi's announcement that he was going into the hills to hunt for game. He fumbled around inside his jeep, emerged with a shotgun, started up a near-by path, and in a few moments disappeared over the hump of a hill. There was a pause. Then two sharp blasts erupted from the hills and filled the valley below with their crashing sound. In a few moments the hunter reappeared over the hill. Smiling sheepishly, Father came toward us, carrying a shotgun in one hand and holding up a dead pigeon with the other. Father Giupponi magnanimously left the pigeon with us for our lunch, got behind the wheel of his jeep, and with a wave of his hand started off down the road in the direction of Chinju.

Damiano and I were lodged in one room of a hut belonging to his aunt and uncle. The walls were made of pressed mud, the roof of thatched rice-straw. One cannot imagine life being more elemental than it is in Korea: it has been reduced to its simplest form of food, shelter, and clothing.

There was no furniture in the house where we stayed; one sits on the floor and meals are brought in—already prepared—on a very low, small table. There were no beds—at night one sleeps between two quilts spread out on the floor. Most of the people possess just one change of clothing. The normal everyday diet consists of a monotonous repetition of rice, soup, and *kimchi,* (a pickled cabbage) resembling sauerkraut. When times are tough—which in the villages is more often than not—barley is substituted for rice.

The weather was pleasantly fresh; the sky overhead was a rich, unclouded blue, and it was a delight to walk through the fields and along the pathways of the village observing the adults at their daily tasks and the children at their play. In the early morning I watched the women going to the river's edge to draw fresh drinking water. Later, the same women would return to the same spot bringing vegetables to be washed; and later still one could see them squatting there by the banks of the river of Nam-sa, pounding their clothes white on the flat gray rocks. In the fields I watched the farmers ladling out the night soil on the fresh young barley sprouts. Human fertilizer is in common usage in Korea; it is good for plants, no doubt, but also good for breeding worms with which many of the people are afflicted. Walking out into the hills, I saw little girls picking the sweet spring grass which grew there and from which their mothers would make soup. Boys were gathering pine needles on the mountain slopes which later would be used as fuel to cook the family rice. Coming down from the side of the mountain, I saw a small boy standing knee-deep in the clear cold water of the river searching under dark rocks for the snails and other creeping things which infest the rivers. I saw young men returning from the hills with massive bundles of twigs and branches loaded on their backs, and all day long I passed boys in their early teens carrying huge loads of topsoil and fertilizer on "jiggey" frames strapped to their slender shoulders.

Then I came upon an unloaded jiggey frame standing upright in an open, green field under a big, empty sky, and the thought occurred to me that, if anything was, then this jiggey frame was the symbol of Korea itself. The principal source of power in Korea continues to be muscle power—for the most part, human muscle. The Korean is one of the many peoples on earth still destined to carry loads, and invariably he carries it on a frame strapped to his back. The jiggey frame itself is simple, yet ingenious: it is shaped like the letter "A," made of a special type of wood, and is as old as Korea itself. It has been, and most likely will continue to be, the principal tool of Korea's vast number of movers and carriers.

Everywhere I moved, turned, and went in Nam-sa there were children. The more I talked, joked, and laughed with them, the more convinced I became that they are far and away Korea's most precious treasure. They are completely unself-conscious, unspoiled, unsophisticated youngsters who are physically beautiful and blessed with the sunniest of dispositions. The parents surround them with measureless warmth and affection. In such an atmosphere the children would become unbearably spoiled and pampered were it not for the normal physical difficulties in their lives which provide a natural built-in set of disciplines, checks, and balances.

The night, the beautiful Korean night, brings to the village a silence and peace which are almost infinite. A breathless stillness settles over everything and the only sounds to be heard are the murmur of conversation and the soft ripple of the swiftly flowing river. There is no electricity in the village and the only light to be seen, other than that given off by moon and stars, is produced by small, dimly burning, peanut-oil lanterns.

On the evening before I left Nam-sa I was invited to one of the larger homes in the village for a soirée of singing, dancing, and storytelling. As many people as could crowded into the house to participate in the festivities. One old gentleman picked up a long stem pipe, took a few puffs, then passed it on to me. I followed his example and the onlookers laughed their approval and delight. At one point in the evening I noticed secret whisperings in a corner of the room, money was seen to change hands, and a boy scurried out on a mission of great importance and urgency. If a few moments he returned carrying a large bottle of rice wine in a big paper bag, and thenceforward the evening proceeded at a more lively pace. The children, sound asleep on the floor, were completely undisturbed by the noise. If they happened to get in the way, their elders would transfer them from one location of the room to another and the children would not so much as blink an eyelash.

Questions were asked concerning my religion: Who was Christ? When did he live? What doctrine did he teach? Is it true that Catholic priests do not marry? How is it possible for them to live such a life?

Other questions were put to me concerning the country of my birth: Is it true that everyone in America is so rich? Is it true that Americans kiss so much?

One old granny told of the time she visited her daughter-in-law in Taegu. Her daughter-in-law insisted upon taking her to see an American movie. "It cost 100 hwan," she said. "Imagine, 100 hwan! The people were as tall as bamboo shoots, their faces were as large as the side of a house, and all they did for one hour was kiss. Kiss and embrace, for one whole hour—ooh, it gave me a bad headache."

Then the village storyteller rose. The room grew quiet, and the children's eyes grew large and bright with expectancy. With vivid facial expressions and eloquent gestures he began to tell the story of the woodsman and the tiger:

"A long time ago in the mountains of North Korea there lived a woodsman. While working in the forest one day, he was attacked by a huge tiger. The woodsman seized the tiger by the tail, and the tiger began turning around in circles, trying to get his teeth into the woodsman. A Buddhist monk, out for a walk, was attracted by the noise and sauntered over. The woodsman, upon seeing the monk, cried out, 'Please take my ax there and kill this tiger before I am eaten alive.' The monk, lowering his eyes and piously folding his hands, replied, 'I am sorry but I cannot kill the tiger. You see, I am a Buddhist and as a Buddhist all life is sacred to me, be it insect, human, or animal.' The woodsman answered, 'Fortunately, I am not blessed with your belief so would you please take my place at the tail of the tiger and let me kill the beast.' The monk agreed and they exchanged places. The woodsman then walked over, picked up his ax, placed it on his shoulder, and nonchalantly strolled off into the forest. The Buddhist monk, very much alarmed, cried out, 'Please, come back and kill this tiger as you promised. Else I will be devoured.' The woodsman's parting reply was: 'I was so impressed by your example that I have become a convert to your belief.'"

The warmth and humor of these simple but sharp-witted country folk was communicative. I felt at ease among them and was sorry when the evening finally came to a close.

It had been decided that Damiano's cousin, who had just turned sixteen, would return to Pusan with us. The lad's mother had already seen two of her sons leave for the cities in search of work, security, and a full belly. She had seen them off and had heard nothing of them or from them since. Now a third son was about to leave. She looked at him sadly for a moment, then said: "Son, do not forget your mother as your brothers have."

The bus came, and we climbed aboard. In a few moments Nam-sa was just a speck far down the dusty road—and a happy memory.

CHAPTER FIVE

THE STORY of the beginnings of the Catholic Church in Korea is unique in the annals of mission history. The Christian faith was introduced into Korea, not by foreigners, but by Koreans themselves; not by missionary priests, but by lay apostles.

In the seventeenth and eighteenth centuries, writings of Jesuit missionaries working in China found their way into Korea. These writings were read with interest and discussed with enthusiasm in certain Korean intellectual circles.

In 1783, Yi Seung Houn, Confucianist scholar, intellectual, and court official, was named a member of the annual Korean delegation sent to the court of Peking to pay tribute to the Chinese Empire. Mr. Yi had a friend who was intensely interested in the writings on Christianity which had trickled into Korea from China, and he asked Yi Seung Houn while in Peking to contact the European scholars who had authored them. "In so doing," the friend said, "you will certainly obtain a quantity of marvelous and interesting objects." He was thinking as much of mathematics as of religion, for the European scholars in question—the Jesuit missionaries—enjoyed at that time widespread renown as mathematicians and astronomers.

So the stage was set for what was to be an historic meeting and an historic conversion. Yi Seung Houn went to Peking, contacted the Jesuit Fathers there, and in the course of his sojourn was instructed and baptized. The first Korean convert was given the name of the first apostle—Peter.

It was a good choice because Peter Yi, upon returning to

Korea in 1785, began immediately to preach the Gospel and to baptize his fellow countrymen. In 1800 the first priest entered Korea. Father James Tchou, Chinese in origin, slipped secretly through the rugged mountain passes of the North and penetrated into the heart of the Hermit Kingdom. Father Tchou was somewhat taken aback to find a fervent group of 4000 baptized and practicing Catholics waiting for him. He was also surprised to find that the Korean Catholics, without benefit of priest, were going to Confession, saying Mass, and administering the other sacraments. All in good faith, of course. Father Tchou quickly put things in order and became the first spiritual shepherd of the fledgling Korean Church.

All went well for a while. Then after a few years the Emperor's police got word that a foreigner preaching a foreign religion was abroad in the land. The police tracked Father Tchou down, arrested him, and put him to death. About the same time, the police ferreted out the nest of Christians which had been giving aid and comfort to Father Tchou—and a bloody persecution was touched off. Eight hundred believers were rounded up and executed; and the soil of Korea had its first taste of the blood of Christian martyrs. It was by no means to be its last.

Later in the nineteenth century, other missionaries followed Father Tchou into Korea. In 1839, three of them—a French bishop and two French priests—were captured in Seoul. After a vicious beating they were beheaded. Another wave of persecutions swept over the country and many new names were added to a now-growing list of Korean martyrs.

About this time a Korean youth by name of Andrew Kim secretly left the country for Macao to begin training for the priesthood. After ordination on August 10, 1845, he smuggled himself back into Korea on a Chinese junk. Father Andrew Kim was working in the North but a short while when his presence was discovered by the local mandarin.

Father Kim was arrested and sent to Seoul, the capital city, to stand trial. There, before a listening tribunal of court officials, he spoke with courage, conviction, and utter disregard for personal safety, of the Christ in whom he believed. The death sentence was passed, and September 16 was set as the day of execution. Father Kim was first stripped of his clothing, then covered with a mixture of water and lime which ate cruelly into his flesh. Finally his head was hacked off by a dancing, fumbling swordsman. He was twenty-six years old. Blessed Andrew Kim, as he is now known, is venerated throughout Korea, and it is hoped that he will soon be canonized.

Twenty years later, in 1865, a third and final persecution broke out. Then the bloody rains ceased, the voice of the turtle was heard in the land, and the Church in Korea was left to continue her work in relative peace.

Why were the Catholics in Korea harassed and persecuted? The reasons were several. First of all, contact with foreigners was illegal, and introduction of outsiders into the Hermit Kingdom was strictly forbidden. Most of all, however, it was a question of rites. Rome had decided that the cult of ancestors and sacrifice to the dead—an integral part of Confucianist ethics—was a form of idolatry; the practice was forbidden to Catholics under pain of mortal sin. It was like forbidding an American today to salute the flag or to stand and take off his hat at the playing of the "Star-Spangled Banner"; because in Korea at that time refusal to perform ancestral rites was tantamount to a grave act of impiety and a serious violation of national ethics. In the minds of the rulers of Korea, then, the Christians were under the sway of foreign ideology and were committing acts which were flagrantly unpatriotic and completely deserving of death. So death was duly meted out—with a vengeance.

It is interesting to note that what Rome forbade in the nineteenth century under pain of mortal sin is considered a perfectly acceptable practice today. Today "ancestor worship" is seen for what it is; namely, a type of innocent respect and reverence for the dead—in no way to be identified with idolatry.

To get back to the persecutions: it was not only a question of fraternizing with foreigners and refusing certain rites, but also a matter of politics. Most of the Catholics in Korea were members of the same political faction, and the opposing political parties seized upon their Christian belief as a good excuse for eliminating them. In so doing, they hoped to advance their own position in the local political arena.

By 1910, when the Japanese seized control of Korea, there were 75,000 Catholics, and over sixty priests—foreign and Korean—in the country. Under the Japanese, Catholics endured much harassment, but no real persecution.

Then came 1950 and the Korean War, and once again the garments of the Bride of Christ in Korea became red with blood. Records are incomplete, but it is known for certain that the Communists put to death five bishops, eighty-two priests, 150 religious and seminarians, and an uncounted number of lay Catholics.

After the Communist War, the Bamboo Curtain dropped with a loud thud across the Thirty-eighth Parallel, and the Church of North Korea became a Church of Silence. Of all the Churches of Silence in the world today, the Church in Communist North Korea is perhaps the most silent. There is absolutely no news of what is going on there, but it is almost certain that not a single priest is active today in all that unhappy land.

The Korean War, which began in 1950 and ended in 1953, was a cataclysm the like of which Korea had never witnessed before. It tore everything up by the roots and left the country ravaged and bleeding from a thousand open wounds. Two million Koreans died in the conflict, either in actual combat or as a result of starvation and exposure brought about by the fighting. Three million Koreans left their ancestral homes and villages in the North and fled south across the Parallel to become refugees. At the end of the war, South Korea had 100,000 orphan children to care for.

Toward the end of the war, there was another phenomenon —this one of a spiritual nature—the like of which Korea had never seen. People began streaming into the churches of Korea, asking for baptism. In the space of only ten years, 1953 to 1963, the number of Catholics in South Korea leapt from 160,000 to 500,000.

In an ordinary city parish, 100 baptisms at Easter or Christmas was not at all an unusual quantity. The number of faithful in a single parish doubled, tripled, quadrupled in as many years. At one time, South Korea could boast the highest number of converts per-number-of-already-existing-Catholics of any country in the world. Today the flow of converts into the Church has slowed, but it has by no means stopped and it may still be accurately termed a "movement."

What is the explanation? I have already mentioned the war—it was definitely a contributing factor. And the postwar period—it, too, played an important part in the convert movement of South Korea. This period—and we are still in it— is characterized by a submarginal standard of existence, by bitter poverty, sickness, death, and insecurity. Many people are groping for something spiritual to sustain them and eventually turn to Christianity. One priest, in preparing a doctoral dissertation on the Church in Korea, put forth the rather interesting thesis that the suicide rate in Korea to some extent parallels its convert rate. That is, in periods of great moral stress, some people are driven to seek release in self-inflicted death and others are driven by the same pressures to embrace religion and spiritual values.

It may also be stated that in modern-day Korea there is a spiritual vacuum. Christianity, so to speak, has the field to itself. There is little or no competition. Buddhism has been the traditional, even official, religion in Korea for centuries— some historians say since the sixth century, others still earlier. Today it still claims 3,000,000 adherents but, practically speaking, it has lost its hold on the people and ceases to be much of a vital force.

Shintoism, animism, and other spiritist sects, beliefs, and superstitions have, at one time or another, enjoyed varying degrees of popularity in Korea. Many of these superstitious beliefs, while still exercising some influence on the daily lives of the people, have lost ground steadily before the inroads of modern science and technology. In mid-twentieth century Korea, such beliefs are generally considered old-fashioned and reactionary.

Confucius also has left an indelible mark on the Korean people. His doctrine, however, is considered more an ethical code than a religion; as such, it lays heavy stress on family morality, respect for authority, and the cult of education and learning. The era of Confucianism is the Old Testament phase of the Korean people; its destiny is to find fulfillment in a New Testament sealed and ratified in the Blood of Christ.

There is not only a spiritual vacuum in Korea, but a cultural one as well. For thirty-six years (1909–45) the Japanese occupied Korea; during this period Korean culture was ruthlessly and systematically wiped out. Today there is a clean slate, a *tabula rasa*.

The impact of Western thought has been felt in Korea, and this, too, has had an unsettling effect upon the minds of the people. They have been cut loose from ancestral moorings and are at present adrift on a strange sea whose tides and currents are unknown to them.

At the everyday, man-in-the-street level there is also void and emptiness. Most of the people live lives of stark poverty. There are few escape mechanisms—no radio, movies, TV, illustrated press, parties, excursions, vacations, and so on. There are few of those diversions and distractions which only money can buy and which people the world over are wont to employ as opiates for the miseries of life. The Korean people, then, stripped of the accidental and contingent, are more open and receptive to the essential and the absolute.

Another very important factor to be considered in a discussion of the convert growth in Korea is the Legion of Mary. In the past, many forms of Catholic Action were tried in Korea. None really worked. Then along came the Legion under the banner of Our Lady and it was found to be ideal for Korea and its problems.

The Legion of Mary was first introduced into Korea in 1955 by a Korean priest on Mokpo Island. It caught on quickly and spread rapidly throughout the ten dioceses of South Korea. The members of the Legion adhere to a rigid, tightly detailed, almost militaristic program which leaves little to chance and even less to arbitrary choice. This serves nicely as an antidote for the irrepressible Korean yen for debate, discussion, and factiousness, which often proved too much for previously tried forms of Catholic Action. It is estimated that one third of the converts in Korea are brought into the Church by members of the Legion of Mary.

◈

CHAPTER SIX

◈

I F, AS HAS BEEN previously stated, one third of the converts in Korea can be attributed to members of the Legion of Mary, another third can be attributed to secondary causes of a less commendable nature, to wit: National Catholic Welfare Conference's relief goods. Any discussion of convert growth in Korea which fails to make mention of this pertinent fact is being neither objective nor intellectually honest.

First, it may be well to describe briefly the conception and execution of N.C.W.C.'s world-wide Catholic Relief Services program. One day shortly after the end of World War II, a priest, sitting in his office in New York City, looked out over the world. He saw, on one hand, that people were hungry everywhere; and, on the other, he saw the government storage bins in the midwest filled to overflowing with surplus food. Everyone is agreed that the best place to store surplus food is in empty bellies. The problem then was one of distribution— how to get the surplus food from the storage bins to the hungry people in question. The priest had a partial answer: through the structural setup of the Catholic Church.

The Church has its dioceses, parishes, and mission stations in every corner of the globe. N.C.W.C. would receive surplus food from the American government and, at the expense of American Catholics, it would organize a staff to supervise handling and shipping. The dioceses and parishes in the poverty-striken reaches of the world would in turn be responsible for final distribution to hungry people: they would be the last—and most important—link in the chain.

It sounds good, and would be good, too—except for one thing. The idea is based on the premise that the priests in the poverty-stricken areas of the world who are on the receiving end of relief goods, who must handle the practical distribution, and, in the final analysis, on whom depends the success or failure of the whole project, think, judge, and act as would American priests in similar circumstances. Such is not the case. American missionaries stationed in these needy areas are comparatively few. The majority are native-born priests—Filipinos, Latin Americans, Africans, Vietnamese, Formosans, and Koreans—or they are other foreign-mission types, such as French, Italian, Irish, Spanish, and so on. Their approach to the problem of relief matériel distribution is not necessarily the same as that of the priest in his New York office who designed the program.

For example, take a typical pastor of a large parish in Korea. He has many expenses to meet: catechists' salaries, church maintenance, building repairs, teaching Sisters' support, etc. His Sunday collection never exceeds twenty-five dollars. The poor pastor's head is aching, and he is at a loss how to make ends meet. Then, of a sudden, as manna from heaven, a big truck marked "N.C.W.C.-C.R.S." pulls up to his church and proceeds to dump on his doorstep $500 worth of cornmeal, white flour, powdered milk, and used clothing. This heart-warming phenomenon is repeated every month, or every few months.

The pastor is told that the relief matériel was donated by the American government and is to be distributed on a needy-only basis. Sure, he understands, and he signs the receipts—in triplicate. But, after all, what is wrong with selling a little to the local merchants and using this money to repair the church roof, pay the catechists, and maintain the parish? He is not using it for himself, mind you, but for the church; and is it not written: "Man does not live by bread alone"? As for the remaining relief goods, well, granted it should be distributed regardless of religion; but a pastor would be less than human if he did not favor first the members of his own congregation. So you have the makings of the *kujei kyou*, or "relief Catholics," as they are known in Korea.

The problem is nothing new: Christ himself had to deal with it in his day. He, also, on at least two different occasions distributed "relief goods" to hungry people in the form of loaves and fishes. The people ate and were satisfied, and, realizing what a good thing they had going for them, rushed to make Christ their king. But Christ fled from them, clearly indicating that he does not desire a faith and love which are bought with bread and fish—or rice—or cornmeal and white flour.

I have seen the problem at work in my own parish in Pusan. When I first came to the parish in 1962, I was delighted to find 200 people enrolled in convert classes. Preliminary detective work revealed, however, that the parish relief program was in something of a mess. One half of the relief goods was being sold to merchants and the money being used for church maintenance. The other half was being distributed to Catholics and catechumens only. This little legerdemain accounted for the exceptionally large number of people under instruction. Little by little the abuses were corrected; the selling stopped, and the food was distributed on a needy-only basis. By the same token, the number of people taking instructions in the parish dwindled from the original 200 to seventy-five. It was something of a shock to the pastor, but one learns quickly in the missions that all that glitters is not gold.

A priest in a neighboring parish had his relief-goods problems also, and one Sunday he decided to meet them head on with an imaginative sermon on the subject. At the Gospel of the Mass, his parishioners were startled to see the two altar boys disappear into the sacristy and emerge a few minutes later dragging a fifty-pound sack of N.C.W.C. cornmeal across the floor of the sanctuary. The pastor opened the sack and, with great aplomb, pulled out a statue of Blessed Andrew Kim, the first Korean martyr. Blessed Andrew was covered with cornmeal from head to toe and, as the pastor began cleaning him off, he explained to the open-mouthed, wide-eyed, neck-straining congregation what he was about.

"At the time of Blessed Andrew Kim," he said, "the Church in Korea was pure and clean and uncontaminated with material things. Its temples were free of buyers and sellers. It served one master: God—not mammon. Now the Church has fallen into the relief-goods business and everywhere relief matériel clings to her. We must cleanse the Church, cast out the buyers and sellers from her temples, and separate her from the mammon of iniquity. In so doing, the Church will once again be pure and spotless as at the time of Blessed Andrew Kim." The sermon is not something one finds in a seminary homiletics textbook but, the pastor assured me, the people got the message—and, in the final analysis, this is what counts.

It must be said, however, that Catholic Relief Services recognizes the problem and has come to grips with it. Parish food programs in Korea have been drastically cut, and there is talk that in the near future they will be stopped altogether. From the viewpoint of the Church it would have been better, perhaps, had they never been begun.

◈

CHAPTER SEVEN

◈

WHAT ARE THE problems facing the Church in Korea today? What are her needs? And what is the outlook for the future?

By and large the problems and needs of the Church in Korea do not differ from those of the Church in other countries: the lay apostolate must be developed; there is room for biblical and liturgical education; the ecumenical movement must be fostered; more priests, sisters, brothers, and lay apostles are needed; and more churches, schools, catechetical centers, and social institutions must be founded. But all these things are peripheral. Paradoxical as it may sound, the *unicum necessarium*, the one essential thing for the Church in Korea today is—poverty: poverty, as lived and preached by Christ; poverty, as extolled in the pages of the Gospels and Epistles and held up as an ideal toward which the Bride of Christ constantly must strive. This ultimately is the pearl of great price. If the Church in Korea discovers it in time, sacrifices her wealth, prestige, and external glory in order to buy it, then the outlook for the future is promising. If not, the outlook is dark and doubtful.

The members of the Church in Korea are drawn almost exclusively from the ranks of the poverty-stricken and destitute. This fact is undeniable. Yet, in all honesty, the Church in Korea cannot be called "the Church of the poor." It takes more—much more—than just a hungry flock to merit that title of glory.

As a matter of record, outside of the government and government agencies (Korean and American), the richest and most powerful institution in South Korea is the Catholic Church. Viewed from without, the Church, in its leaders, its rectories, its churches, its convents, and its general *modus operandi*, does not reflect the poverty and humility of Christ. On the contrary, there is a bit of triumphalism in her make-up, and her face seems set more in the direction of Tabor than of Bethlehem and Calvary. Several concrete examples will help illustrate this point.

Example: A new parish has been established in Pusan in an area which boasts some of the worst slums in South Korea. The pastor recently discovered one family in the parish living in an abandoned Japanese tomb. Many of the parishioners live in hovels worse than the lairs of animals. Yet the church which has risen up out of these slums, and which now discordantly dominates the skyline, would do itself proud in Munich or Minneapolis. It is huge and pretentious, with fancy German architecture, huge windows, and wrought-iron sculpture work. Now an expensive bell tower is being added, like the cherry on a banana split.

Example: A group of Sisters here, living under the vow of poverty and dedicated to the service of the poor, discovered recently that their living quarters were too small and uncomfortable, and so decided to build a new convent. The new convent was designed by a Swiss architect, no less, which would be appropriate if it were located in Zurich or Geneva. Unfortunately it is located in Pusan—in one of the most poverty-depressed cities in the world. There the convent sits today in all its splendor looking out over the sea, rising up layer upon layer like a rich wedding cake. It boasts such deluxe items as a private veranda for each nun's private room. The convent is sometimes mistaken for a resort hotel; it is never taken to be a house for poor women dedicated to serving poor people.

Example: Go to any Buddhist monastery in Korea and what do you find? Monks or nuns, as the case may be, living lives of most austere poverty. No furniture. Coarse clothes. Meatless diet. No wine. They beg for a living. Go to a Catholic monastery in Korea and what do you find? *Korean* monks (I do not refer to the non-Koreans in this comparison) clothed in expensive wool habits, wearing costly leather shoes; using chairs, tables, beds; enjoying central heating, central plumbing, baths, showers, refrigerators, electric fans; eating meat once, twice—sometimes three times—a day; living in spacious, comfortable three-story monasteries. Or go to any one of the three Carmelite convents in Korea. With the money it took to build any one of these, one could easily erect ten Buddhist monasteries accommodating a proportionate number of people. As regards poverty, at least, it would seem the disciples of Christ in Korea have something to learn from the disciples of Buddha.

Example: A Korean priest came to see me recently to solicit help for his new church. "Is your present building too small?" I naïvely asked. "No, but it's too poor and too simple," he replied. "My idea is to tear it down and build something big, attractive, impressive. Then many *nophun sarami* ("high-class people") will come into the Church. If our buildings are too poor and simple, we can never hope to attract the wealthy and the intellectuals."

"Tell me, Father," I ventured, "how do these people, who are drawn to the Church by its rich façade, come to believe in a Christ who was born in a stable and lived as a beggar?" Upon hearing this, Father laughed, threw up his hands in despair, and said, "You do not understand the Korean mind."

One could go on and on—and on. But the point is, these are not isolated examples. Moreover, they reflect a way of thinking and a way of doing which is diametrically opposed to the mind of Christ.

A need for poverty on the missions? Who would believe it! Sounds a little like carrying coals to Newcastle—yet it is so.

One day, while at Louvain, I heard a Chinese bishop, freshly expelled from China, remark somewhat sadly: "The

Communists in China were not a hundred per cent wrong in persecuting the Church, because the Church in China had become one of the richest, most powerful, and most capitalistic institutions in the entire country."

Somewhat in the same vein, not long ago I had occasion to meet an American religious superior whose community of teaching nuns had just returned from Castro's Cuba. Among other things, Sister said: "Unfortunately most of our better Catholic schools in Cuba catered to the rich; the children of the poor were comparatively neglected. Not because we wanted it that way, but because we needed the income which only the rich could provide to support ourselves. Whatever the reason, it made the Church a sitting duck for Communist diatribe and propaganda."

Also, on a trip to Japan a few years ago I met the Japanese Ordinary of a large industrial city. While discussing the problems of his diocese, he remarked with a shrug: "I've been trying for ten years now to persuade one of the many mission groups who work in my diocese to begin a parish in the slums. So far I have been unsuccessful." One of the most damning indictments I have ever heard of Catholic foreign mission activity came from the lips of a Belgian missionary who had been working in North Vietnam and escaped just before the Communist take-over. He said: "There is a saying among the common people of North Vietnam: 'rich as a missionary.'"

There may not be a saying in South Korea, "rich as a missionary," but the church here projects a general image of wealth, power, and prestige—as opposed to poverty, humility, and service. If the Communists were to take over South Korea, they would find the Church here—as in China and Cuba—a ready target for their attacks.

What steps must be taken then for the Church in South Korea to become "the Church of the poor"—not just numerically but spiritually and *really* as well? There is basically but one step, and it consists in imitating the example of

Christ. The leaders of the Church in Korea must identify themselves with the poor of the land just as Christ un-equivocally identified himself with the poor of Palestine. The bishops, priests, and sisters must live lives of poverty—not episcopal poverty, clerical poverty, or religious poverty, which is often antiseptic, germ-free, and really not too uncomfortable: but *poor-man* poverty, such as Christ lived and which will be accepted as such by the man in the street without explanation or apology.

Of course it is not possible for the non-Korean priest or sister in Korea to live exactly as do the poor of the land: one would last about two weeks. The important thing, however, is that one work in this direction, that one try, that one be possessed of a will-to-be-poor. If such be the case, it is really surprising how far one can go in the direction of poverty without ever overstepping his own physical or psychological limitations. It is equally surprising how eloquently one can preach the poverty and humility of Christ by his own external comportment and mode of living without sacrificing in the least mental or bodily health, provided only that one be possessed of the all important will-to-be-poor.

The Church not only in its personnel but in its buildings as well must convey the double idea of poverty and service rather than of pomp and prestige. Its churches must truly give the impression of being houses of the poor rather than the exteriorization of some pastor's ego. Her convents and rectories must be designed with utmost simplicity and austerity. They must be able to withstand the scrutiny of the Christ whose taste in religious architecture runs in the general direction of stables and workmen's cottages.

Not only must the Church be poor: she must also go to the poor. As Christ, her Master, the Church must go first and foremost not to the politicians, the intellectuals, the people of means and power—the elite—but to the most poverty-stricken, the most helpless, the most needy. To such as these she must distribute the riches of Christ's truth and love. If the

Church in this parched and poverty-stricken peninsula of South Korea realizes in time her vocation and truly becomes "the Church of the poor," then she has nothing to fear for the future; the Poorman of Nazareth will be with her always and the gates of hell—and Moscow, and Peking, and Hollywood—will not prevail against her.

CHAPTER EIGHT

MICHAEL RHI WAS in his early twenties. He was a sharp dresser and much concerned with his personal appearance. Shoes highly polished, pants freshly creased, a crisp white shirt, carefully knotted tie, and his dark black hair well groomed and oiled—he had the reputation among his friends of being a *motjaengi* (a dandy). His facial expression was alert and sensitive, and his features appeared sharper and more Western-like than those of most Koreans. His complexion was the color of wax and his dark melancholy eyes had a quality of the dreamer and poet about them.

I had seen Michael around the Central Church, and on a number of occasions had passed the time of day with him. He sang in the church choir and was also a member of the Legion of Mary. I also met him at a wedding feast to which I had been invited. He was called upon to sing and acquitted himself very well, singing "Danny Boy," "O Sole Mio," and another song, in a true, rich tenor voice.

One afternoon, as is my wont sometimes, I stopped by the Classical Music Hall. Michael Rhi was there at the time. He was sitting on the edge of a chair in a corner of the room, elbows resting on his knees and chin cupped in his hands. He was far off and away in outer space somewhere, borne on the wings of beautiful music. He noticed me looking his way, returned to earth with something of a start, smiled a nervous greeting, then sat upright in his chair. He glanced a few times in my direction, rather furtively I thought. Then he got up and, picking his way through several rows of chairs, came over to me. He smiled a slightly embarrassed, self-conscious smile and asked if he could see me sometime.

Sure. Anytime. How about tonight?

That would be fine, he said. He would come at seven-thirty. He thanked me, then nervously made his exit from the hall.

When he first entered my room he began with forced brightness to speak of inconsequential things: the weather; how does Father like Korea?; an American movie (*The Sun Also Rises*) now playing at a downtown theater; the latest police crackdown on draft dodgers; and so on. Under the surface of his words I could detect violent emotion and feeling crying out to be released.

Then with no transition at all Michael began to speak his mind. Like infected matter from a pierced abscess, his pent-up thoughts poured out almost compulsively in bitter monologue.

"To live in Korea today," he began, "is tragedy. You know what I mean? Like in Shakespeare—comedy and tragedy. Well, to live in Korea is a great tragedy. Most of the people have no work and no food. You need eyes like a cat to stay alive, to be cunning and shrewd like a cat; to outwit your neighbor, to get money.

"Look at me. Clean shirt, tie, shined shoes; my friends think I am very prosperous boy. Ha, that is a joke. My friends see me in the street and they say 'Have you eaten your rice?' And I say, 'Yes, everything is peaceful.' If they really knew my poor condition they could not believe it. I have pride and would rather die than let them know.

"My family is from the North and once we were prosperous people. Then the Communist war broke out and my family fled south. My father was killed. The rest of my family came to Pusan. At that time there were many refugees in Pusan; we had no place to stay. So we built a home from canvas on the city dump and we are still there now.

"I spent all New Year's night in Classical Music Hall, weeping over my sad life. I cannot live without music—Mozart, Chopin, Beethoven. Especially do I like Beethoven. Do you know his Fifth Symphony? Da-da-da dum, da-da-da dum. I like that most of all. I know the girl who works in Classical Music Hall, she is kind and lets me in without paying. I spend most of my time there now. Sometimes I do not think it is good because it makes me sad. New Year's Eve, the whole night I cry.

"When I graduate from high school I am number-three boy in class of 500. All my teachers, they tell me: 'Go to the university.' Father, this country and nation give to me my life. When I die my bones will be buried in this soil. I am Korean and I wish to help them. I wanted to go to college but I am prevented by the poor circumstances of my life.

"I look to find job, but no job. Especially for boy like me. I am frail and weak. Look, my body is like that of child, like that of baby. My body is so thin that I think I must die."

Saying this he extended his arm, took my hand in his, and placed it about his wrist, wanting me to confirm what he had just said. Then he released my hand and continued speaking:

"The night is my enemy. I do not sleep. I lie in bed with eyes open thinking, always thinking about my sad life. In the morning I wake up and everything is black. I ask to myself, 'What shall I do today? . . . and tomorrow—and for the rest of my life?'

"In the morning I eat my rice with head down, not even looking up at my mother and sister. Sometimes in the morning I break things, I beat my head against the wall, I throw things. Like an animal. When I can get wine from my friends, I drink. . . .

"The Church tells me to pray. Pray, that's fine. Tell me this: how can I pray when my belly is empty? Tomorrow maybe I will be dead. Then I go to heaven and when I am in heaven, then I pray.

"Sometimes, Father, I think maybe I lose my mind."

I asked when was the last time he had eaten anything. This morning he had a bowl of rice, he said, nothing else since.

I opened my desk drawer, counted out some hwan notes,

wrapped them in a piece of newspaper, and handed them to Michael. I told him that a friend in America had sent me a little money and requested that I give it to someone in need.

Michael stared at the package which I held out to him and on his face I could read the conflict which raged inside. He pushed my hand away, buried his face in his hands, and began sobbing. His thin shoulders shook and his whole body was wracked by a dry, painful, choked sobbing. Finally he said:

"Father, I am not a beggar."

I placed the money in his shirt pocket, held back the hand which reached up to remove it, and told him that the money was his by right; forget about it. I also told him to buy himself a good meal, try to get a good night's sleep, and maybe we could talk things over again sometime. He started to protest again, but instead smiled like a little boy, wiped his eyes unashamedly with his handkerchief, thanked me, and said that he would like to see me again. Then he carefully put on his shoes and was gone.

In the weeks and months that followed I saw much of Michael Rhi. One day he asked me very shyly if I would not like to visit his home in Tent City. I said I would like that very much.

It had been raining all morning, but at noon the rain subsided and the clouds disappeared. By the time we started out across town in the direction of Tent City a cold sun was shining down from a hard, clear blue sky. Arriving at Tent City, however, I was dismayed to see that the morning rains had transformed the entire area into a sea of ankle-deep mud and muck. I rolled up my trouser cuffs and, following Michael's example, waded in. The soft black slime oozed over our shoe tops and we had to pick our way along carefully.

Michael explained to me that ten years ago the area over which we were now passing had been part of the Bay of Pusan. Dirt, garbage, trash, and refuse, however, continued to be dumped here until the water's edge gradually receded and eventually gave way to dry ground. In turn the dry ground was soon overrun by a city of tents. Now 4000 people call the area home.

Most of the people earn their living, at least in part, by scavenging in the refuse for paper, junk, and food: anything that is salvageable, salable, or edible.

Everywhere there were women, children, and men: scraping, rooting, sorting, and piling. I watched one woman pick up a dirty apple core from the muck, wipe it off carefully on her sleeve, and then eat it. I saw another woman, with a baby on her back, pick up a soggy crust of bread and place it in her blouse, apparently to eat later when it was dry.

As we approached the particular area where his family lived, Michael began a rapid flow of talk.

"Father, my house is so poor that I am ashamed to bring you here, such a hovel you have never seen. It is so miserable that perhaps we should go back. . . ."

I made a few reassuring sounds to dispel Michael's mounting uncertainty and at the same time quickened my pace, more impatient than ever to escape from the cold wind which had begun to blow in from the bay. Finally Michael held back and pointed timidly to a shack at the end of the alley, and I understood that this was it. Home. It was slapped together with canvas, tar paper, cardboard, and old lumber. It differed in no way from the other dwellings of Tent City. Twelve feet long and perhaps ten feet wide; this was home for Michael, his mother, three brothers, and two sisters.

I followed Michael inside and he introduced me to his mother, who had been expecting us. Mrs. Rhi pulled two cushions out from a pile of blankets and quilts in the corner and placed these on the floor for Michael and me to sit on. Mrs. Rhi remained standing.

The room was quite cold and the wind seemed free to come and go as it pleased through the cracks and openings in the canvas. On the wall behind Mrs. Rhi hung a small, pink plastic crucifix and a few pious images, which Michael, the only Catholic in the family, had placed there.

Michael's eyes slid over the dingy living quarters; then looking down at the floor he smiled in that hesitant, self-conscious way of his and asked, "Well, what do you think of it?" "It's nice," I said. "Clean."

Mrs. Rhi wanted to tell me about Il-sun, her oldest son and the firstborn male in the family, who always enjoys a privileged position in Oriental society. As she began speaking, a thin veil of tears covered her dark eyes and the already present lines of grief in her face seemed to deepen.

Il-sun had just turned twenty-six. Always a little more sensitive than the other Rhi children, he was the most affected by the submarginal standard of living which they were forced to live. Finally something snapped inside and two years ago Il-sun suffered a major breakdown.

"Garbage-dump neurosis," interjected Michael.

Mrs. Rhi ignored the interruption and continued her story. At first, she said, she sent Il-sun to a mental institution which provided room and board, but no medical care. After a while even this proved too expensive and Il-sun was forced to return home. Upon his return Il-sun proceeded to erect a small, kennel-like, cardboard structure in the anteroom just outside the main room of the tent. He established living quarters there, cutting himself off from the rest of the family. He seldom leaves this shelter except to fetch the food which his mother places near the entrance, or to take care of his bodily needs.

After she finished talking, Mrs. Rhi went out of the room and began speaking to Il-sun in his box. She wanted him to meet me. Finally she enticed him outside and we exchanged a few words with him. He is obviously mentally sick, but it is difficult to say how badly.

After saying good-by to the Rhi family, I went with Michael to call upon the mayor of Tent City. We found him at home, busy sorting and piling scrap iron in a corner of his tent.

We talked for a while. Then I asked him how his people managed to stay alive in Tent City.

"Well," answered the mayor, "it's not easy to starve to death

in Korea. Besides what we pick up in the trash heap, we have
the American relief material: cornmeal, white flour, powdered
milk, and canned cheese. But once we're sick—we're dead."

As the weeks passed, Michael became a source of growing
concern and worry to me. Each time he came to see me he
looked more pale and emaciated.

Many times, he told me, he didn't bother to eat, going
whole days sometimes on just a bowl of rice and bit of soup.
I told him he must eat if he wants to live. He just shrugged his
shoulders and replied that the food was so tasteless and insipid
that it held little attraction for him. If he happened to be at
home at mealtime and someone placed a bowl of rice before
him he would eat. Otherwise he wouldn't bother.

Michael spent the year following his graduation from high
school working as a houseboy at the American army compound
near Pusan. During this period of time he was given American
food to eat: meat, milk, desserts, bread, butter, coffee, sugar,
and so on. After that he found he had little appetite for rice
and seaweed soup. He was sorry to leave the American base,
but there was a reduction in personnel and he was forced to
go.

Michael was convinced that if members of the Korean Army
were served the same food as the American GI every youth in
Korea would enlist tomorrow. In speaking of the contrast between the American way of life and the Korean struggle for
existence, Michael offered up the following tidbits:

"In America people ask themselves the question: how can I
make my body thin? In Korea people ask the question: how
can I make my body fat?

"In America people wake in the morning and they ask: how
can I make my life more enjoyable today? In Korea people
wake in the morning and ask: how can I stay alive today?

"In America medicine consists of drugs and antibiotics. In
Korea medicine is to suffer and to endure."

This type of comparison was Michael's trademark. Sometimes I thought he spent his nights dreaming them up. Along these same lines, he remarked to me one day:

"In America and Europe people meet each other and they say: Hello, good morning. In Korea people meet each other and they say: Have you eaten your rice? This is the important thing in our living, whether we eat or do not eat. Beside this, nothing is important."

Michael started talking one day about the American GIs in Korea. Placing himself in the role of a GI, he spit his words out contemptuously and bitterly:

"Korea, ha, is nothing but land of slicky boys, land of prostitutes. You gooks will never amount to anything. Can a rose blossom in a trash heap?

"When I was working at the American army base, do you know what I see written in one of the barracks? It is written on large cloth sign and hung in center of wall. It is this: 'If you have been in Korea you will go to heaven when you die because you have already served your time in hell.' Also I see written on the back of jackets worn by some GIs: 'Korea—the land that God forgot.' This is what the GI thinks of us gooks."

There is a lot of truth in what Michael had to say. At present there are 50,000 American servicemen in Korea, all counting the days until their tour of duty is up. For the most part, Koreans are poor and destitute, their land is bleak and rugged; and the GI upon arriving here is convinced he has reached the ragged edge of the universe.

Korea is considered one of the most undesirable assignments in the American Army. It is called a "hardship tour."

I have visited military bases in Korea on a number of occasions. I still haven't been able to figure out where the hardship part comes in. Imported American food—the best—is served up in abundant quantity at each meal. To supplement this there is the ubiquitous, well-stocked commissary and PX, offering everything from the latest edition of *Playboy* Magazine to frozen turkeys, often at cut-rate prices. There are bars and dance halls, there are libraries, movie theaters, television broad-

casting studios, bowling alleys, swimming pools, and gymna-
siums. There are special resort facilities, beach clubs, and craft
shops. The whole bit. And all the dirty work—the moving
and carrying, the scrubbing and cleaning, the hauling of garbage and the shining of officers' boots—all this is done by
Korean employees.

And to while away the long leisure hours for the American
serviceman who is proudly serving his God and his country on
freedom's far-flung frontier in order to make the world safe for
democracy—there are the girls. Tens of thousands of them,
yanggongjus, or "yankee princesses," as they are called. One
Maryknoll Father whose parish is near a large American military
compound told me that there were 6000 "princesses" in his parish alone.

As Michael further pointed out to me, unfortunately most
GIs never get to know the true Korea. All they see of it are its
two worst elements, the "slicky boys" and the prostitutes. As a
result, they often have nothing but spit and dust for the country
and an attitude of superiority toward the people.

Michael was the only member of the Rhi family who was a
Catholic. He was very devoted to his mother and many times
he asked me to come to his home to "convert" her. The
naïveté of this request amused me. At Michael's repeated in-
sistence, however, I finally gave way and paid a second visit to
Tent City, this time to "convert" Mrs. Rhi.

Michael's mother said that, yes, she felt a great need for religion in her life. She used to be a Buddhist, but now Buddhism
had no attraction for her. Mrs. Rhi would like to come to the
church and study the teachings of Christ; but later, not now.

When questioned about this, Mrs. Rhi at first answered only
with an embarrassed silence. I said that I was sorry if I had
asked a personal question.

No, she said softly, it wasn't that. It was true that she would
like to learn about Christ and that she felt a need for God in
her life. But at present there was only one thing on her
mind: to find food and money for her family. If her economic

situation improved and her mind was more at rest, then she would come to the church and study Christian doctrine.

Mrs. Rhi may not be Christian but in many respects her attitude was very Christ-like. Her children frequently would bring home orphan waifs and beggars picked up in the streets whom she would feed and clothe. As a matter of fact the whole family seemed to have inherited the mother's generous heart.

Michael told me of his sister who was sent on an errand by her father to the other side of Pusan. She was waiting on the street corner for the bus which was to take her home, clinging tightly to the thirty hwan which she had been given for carfare. She noticed an old beggar sitting on the opposite side of the street, looking very sad and forlorn. Moved by pity, she crossed over, gave her thirty hwan to the old man, and then proceeded to walk the three or four miles home. Michael related that she was completely exhausted when she arrived home; I could readily believe it, for she is just a wisp of a girl and seems quite frail.

During my second visit to Tent City, Michael asked if I wished to hear about something which had occurred to him recently. I said that I did.

The Korean language and mode of expression is drawn up so as to cushion the shock of direct encounters between individuals; as a matter of fact it sometimes takes two or three sentences just to say "yes" or "no." So when Michael had something to say it usually took him two or three paragraphs to work up to it. After this preliminary question-and-answer period, in which I assured Michael that I did most certainly want to hear what he had to say; that, no, it would not take up too much of my time; that even if I did not approve of what he told me I still would be most interested to hear about it, he finally got to the point.

"Yesterday evening," he began, "I was leaving the church and coming home. It was getting dark. I turned a corner of the street and walked down a side alley. I fell over a beggar who was lying there in the alley and whom I did not see.

"There are many beggars in Pusan and you learn to pay them no attention, so I hurried on my way. Then I began to think, I thought of your words, 'Christ identifies himself with the poor, Christ lives in the poor.' I stopped and went back to the beggar. I do not know why I did this but sometimes I am a funny boy. I knelt beside the beggar in the alley and lifted up his head. He opened his eyes and looked at me. He looked weak and sick.

"I smelled his breath but there was no smell of wine. He was in rags and dirty, but I don't know, he was not like other beggars I see in Pusan. There was something different about him. He seemed very young and like gentle boy. I asked him if he was sick and he told me he was hungry. His speech was not like beggar but like high-class man, like boy who has been to college. I helped the beggar to his feet, gave him the 500-hwan bill which you gave me a few days ago, and told him to buy some food. I watched him go into a restaurant. He looked very bad and weak and I think he will die soon. Maybe the food he can buy with the money will keep him alive a few more days."

After recounting this episode, Michael asked my opinion on what he had done. Had he acted wisely? After all, he said, that money should have been given to his family. Moreover, he had foolishly recounted the episode about the beggar to his cousin, and his cousin was furious, accusing him of lightheadedness and the worst kind of folly. I told him that he had done well and he seemed somewhat reassured by this.

I tried to obtain work for Michael Rhi at the American army base in Pusan. At one time I thought I had succeeded, but what at first looked like success turned out to be just another disappointment in a long line of disappointments for Michael.

I received a phone call from the sergeant in charge of Special Services at Hialeah Compound. The chaplain had spoken to him about Michael, and the sergeant told me that if Michael were a good singer and knew English songs there might—just might—be an opening for him with the Korean band which plays nightly at the Starlite Club on the base. At any rate, if Michael were interested he should come out to audition with the Korean band and give it a try.

Michael hurried out to the army base in the afternoon, all aflutter with excitement and expectancy. After waiting around for a few hours he was finally permitted to sing a few songs at the band rehearsal. After the audition he was told to be on hand at the Starlite Club at 8 P.M.

Things did not go too well at the Starlite Club. First of all, Michael had never sung with a band before. This in itself created quite a problem. Secondly, his English repertory consisted solely of ballads and semi-classical tunes. The Americans, it seemed, wanted jazz, country 'n western, rock 'n roll, and pop. Also, Michael got into a hot argument with the band leader and this certainly didn't help matters any. At any rate, when Michael left the Starlite Club with his night's pay of 500 hwan, he was coolly informed that his services were no longer needed. Upon hearing this, hot tears spurted from his eyes and he gave way to complete discouragement.

I told Michael I would keep trying at the base and sooner or later something would turn up, a job as translator, clerk, houseboy, something. He seemed to take little consolation from these vague promises.

Whenever Michael came to see me I would try to have something on hand to give him to eat: crackers, a candy bar, a can of peaches, or something of this nature. However, after his failure at the Starlite Club, which in context was a traumatic experience for him, he became so dejected and depressed that he would accept nothing. He would repeat many times what had become his popular refrain: "If I could die studying—I would die happy!"

I would have liked nothing better than to send Michael to the university, but how could I? The little money I had upon my arrival in Korea did not last long. One comes into contact with so much misery here that it is difficult to hang on to much capital for any length of time.

Michael, almost in tears one evening, insisted that his life was "cursed by God." Everything I do, he said, turns into failure and disappointment. He brought up again the subject of suicide, or "self-murder," as he called it. He had spoken about this many times before, but I never took him seriously. Now for the first time he gave the impression that he meant what he said.

"Every time I pass a car or a truck," he said, "I must hold myself back. I'm afraid I will throw myself in front of it and kill myself. My mother knows my thoughts. Always at home now she looks at me very worried. When I leave home she asks where I go. Sometimes she sends my younger brother and sister to watch me."

I spoke to him for a long time. He just stared at the floor and said nothing.

After his misadventure at the Starlite Club, Michael seemed to slide deeper and deeper into melancholy, apathy, and depression. He spoke more frequently of "self-murder." He also talked of enlisting in the army. "If I do not do something soon," he would say, "I will lose my mind."

One morning I asked about his health. He remarked: "Lately something strange takes place. In the morning I put handkerchief to my mouth and when I take it away it is wet with blood."

"Does this happen every day?"

"Not every day, but usually. It has been like this for two weeks now."

"How about fever?" I asked. "At night do you sweat very much?"

"Yes, sometimes."

I thought for a moment; then I asked Michael the cost of a lung X-ray. Specifics of this kind seem to be common knowledge among the poor and Michael told me quickly that it would cost 4000 hwan (four dollars). Okay, I said, take this money, have your chest X-rayed, and return here when the pictures are developed. He took the money and left with no more concern than if he had been sent to the post office to buy some stamps.

I put on my hat and coat, slipped on my shoes at the door, and started over toward the Maryknoll Sisters' Dispensary. It is a seven-minute walk from the bishop's house. I entered by the main gate, turned left through the garden, past the gold-fish pond, and then past a long line of sick people who were waiting patiently on wooden benches. The place was a bee-hive of ordered activity. Names were being called out, nurses were flitting to and fro carrying medicines or sick babies, and patients were going in and out of the wooden dispensary buildings, holding slips of paper in their hands.

I stopped one of the nurses I saw and asked to see Sister Gilmary. I was told to wait. In a few minutes Sister Gilmary appeared, tall, lanky, dressed in white, and smiling pleasantly. Sister is a medical doctor; she is also in charge of the clinic's TB section.

I explained why I had come. Sister told me that their TB program was geared to handle only a hundred patients. These must live in a prescribed area in the vicinity of the clinic in order that their treatment may be supervised in their homes. The sisters have scarcely enough food and medicine to treat this number and, as it is, the quota is already completely filled and there is a long waiting list. However, if I could return with Michael and the X-ray in the afternoon, she would be happy to look at him and to prescribe treatment.

I was back again in the afternoon with Michael and the X-ray. After a twenty-minute wait, we were shown into Sister's minuscule office.

Sister told Michael to strip to the waist. She examined him first with a stethoscope, then, placing one hand flat on various parts of his chest and shoulders and tapping on the back of this hand with the fingers of the other hand, she held her ear close, listening attentively. In the strong light pouring through the window in Sister's office, Michael looked so thin and ema-ciated as almost to be transparent. Sister asked Michael a number of questions. Then she removed the X-rays from the large manila envelope, held them up to the light, and began scrutinizing them from every angle. Then she asked Michael, who was tucking his shirt back into his trousers, to wait outside. Michael appeared lighthearted and even seemed to enjoy the attention which was being paid him.

After Michael had left, Sister turned to me and said:

"Well, he's got it all right, and it's bad enough. His right lung is only slightly tainted and spotty, but his left lung is seriously infected. With proper medicine and complete rest it will prob‐ably be two years before he recovers."

I asked her to write down the name of the medicine and vitamins he should have. Sister began writing on a small scrap of paper, at the same time keeping up a steady flow of talk.

"If you wish to help him, Father, you must impress upon him the need for absolute rest. Otherwise you are wasting your efforts. The Koreans have many qualities, but when it comes to treating themselves for TB they are like children. They rest and take medicine for a month, maybe two. Then they feel miraculously better and hop out of bed and start moving about. Two or three months later the relapse sets in, and they are knocked flat on their backs and are much worse than before. To recover fully takes much time, much patience, and com‐plete rest. The patients on our program receive food and med‐icine twice a week in their homes; however, if we were to visit a home and find the patient absent, he would automatically be cut from the program. This may seem harsh, but it is the only way. We have so little food and medicine here to work with that it would be quite foolish to pour what little we have down the drain."

Sister handed me the paper on which she had been writing and assured me that if Michael took the medicine and vitamin pills, rested, and ate properly, it was as much as she or anyone else could do to help him. She also told me to have him re‐port to the clinic in six months and she would have another look at him. I thanked her and left.

On the way back, a light rain began to fall. Michael rolled up the manila envelope containing the X-rays and carefully tucked it inside his jacket. The X-rays had cost 4000 hwan, a vast sum in Korea, and they were not to be treated lightly.

After we had stepped into my room, Michael removed the envelope, unrolled it on the bed, and began smoothing it out, running the palms of his hands over it. Seeing that there were a few dark splotches of moisture on it, he placed it on the end of the bed, closer to the stove.

Michael still had an air of complete unconcern about him. He seemed utterly devoid of any doubt or suspicion, or even interest, regarding the day's proceedings.

I told Michael what the doctor had told me. He had tuberculosis and it would be two years, maybe more, before he could hope for complete recovery. I wanted very much to be gentle, but my words—even to me—sounded short and sharp.

Michael was stunned. His eyes grew wide, his jaw dropped slightly, and his face registered at first disbelief, then terror.

"Is it very bad?" he asked.

"It's bad enough," I answered. "The doctor thinks it will take possibly two years before complete recovery."

He buried his face in his hands and began swaying back and forth, groaning softly to himself: "A-eee-go, a-eee-go, a-eee-go. . . ."

For fully three minutes neither one of us said a word. When Michael finally looked at me, hot tears were streaming down his cheeks, and he made no effort to hide them. Then his mouth tightened, his face grew hard, and he began to speak in a cool, deliberate, and frighteningly bitter voice.

"*Sinbunim malsum jom mulopopsita.*" (May I ask a question of you?)

"Yes."

"Please answer me this: Is God charity, or is God cruelty? . . . If God is charity, how can he do this to me?"

His words were meant to hurt, and they did. I made no attempt to answer them. I began speaking to Michael about the practical measures to be taken to cure his sickness. First of all, he should get away from Pusan and the foul, germ-infested air of its factories and slums. I asked him if he had any relatives who lived in the mountains or near the sea who would be willing to lodge him for six months or a year. He answered that he had some distant cousins who lived in a small village near Inchon. The village was close to the sea, where the air was good. Perhaps he could go there.

Next I asked him to prepare a list with the cost of food, medicine, and transportation needed for a period of six months. I told him to bring this list back in a few days and we would try to work something out together. As he was leaving he thanked me and even managed to force a smile. Underneath he looked rather dazed.

A week later Michael returned with the list which I had asked him to prepare. It was written carefully in ink on the reverse side of a used envelope. It read as follows:

Necessaries of living for TB boy (six months)

Eating	rice and side dishes	20,000 hwan
	1 apple for each day	4,000 hwan
Medicaments	TB pills	10,000 hwan
	vitamins	10,000 hwan
Transportation	rail train to Inchon from Pusan (3 class)	8,000 hwan
		52,000 hwan (52 dol)

It was less than I had anticipated. As I studied the list, Michael began to mumble something in an apologetic tone of voice. At first it was rather garbled and I didn't understand what he was talking about. Then I realized he was talking about apples. He was apologizing for his rashness in placing an apple a day on the list of "necessaries."

After all, he explained, an apple was a luxury and he really did not need it. But his stomach was so bad now and his digestion so poor that an apple was a big help each day. But if I did not approve, he said, it was all right to cross it from the list.

I assured him that I understood. Then I asked if he had received a reply from his cousin. Yes, it was all arranged. When would he be ready to leave? This evening, tomorrow morning, now—anytime.

I gave Michael the money and then proceeded to lecture him like a Dutch uncle on the necessity of resting, of patience, of cheerful thinking. So forth and so on. Even then I had the feeling I was wasting my time. He was of the sick, I was of the healthy; and a vast chasm lay between our respective worlds. It would take more than words to bridge that chasm and establish communication.

Michael decided to leave Pusan on the next train. He thanked me extensively, asked to be remembered in my prayers, promised solemnly to take care of himself, assured me that he would write often, shook hands, and was gone.

Some time later I received a letter postmarked "Inchon." It was from Michael, and he wrote as follows:

Dear So Sinbunim,
Jhanmi Jesus. (Praise be Jesus.)
The smell of the sea is in the air and the waves break rhythmically on the rocky shore.

I arrived here at Inchon many weeks ago and have been resting in the room of house which belongs to cousin. . . . I am very lonely in the country. I live with relatives. In the early morning they go out to the fields and I do not see them again until late in evening. I sleep in room by myself but it is so lonely that I cannot sleep. I am not used to sleeping in room with no one else in it and I do not enjoy it.

My only companion here has been small puppy dog but he is gone now. Dog meat is good for TB patient and last week I killed the dog and make soup. Now his flesh is part of my flesh.

I wish to thank Father again for his help. It is very difficult for me to speak of my needs. Koreans are proud and I am trembling with shame when I receive money from you to help cure my TB sickness. It would be easier to cut arm off than to accept help from someone. I am not beggar.

My body remains for me great evil. Always I am exhausted, I digest poorly, and I sleep little. I take the medicine which I brought with me and I no longer spit blood, which is an improvement. In school the teacher once told our class, "A healthy mind in a healthy body." This makes me laugh because my mind becomes diseased with my body.

I have two years of this to look forward to—and then after that, what? I cannot hope to complete studies so I have the choice of being soldier, beggar, or ragpicker.

In Pusan I could listen to beautiful music in the homes of friends or in Classical Music Hall. Music is necessary for my soul as rice is for my body, but here there is no music— only the insects and the wind. Some nights I go for long walks along the seashore, and this brings me peace.

Please pray to St. Mary for me.

        Rhi Ki Young (Michael)

More than two months went by with no news from Michael. Then one morning, as I was shaving before Mass there was an unexpected knock on the door of my room. It was six o'clock in the morning and I couldn't imagine who would be calling at that hour.

I opened the door and there was Michael Rhi. He looked weak, exhausted, feverish, and slightly demented. I told him to come in and he did so without even taking off his shoes. He sat down on a chair, closed his eyes, leaned his head back, and breathed in and out gaspingly through his mouth.

After a while he began to speak, rather haltingly and incoherently, but the meaning of what he said was clear enough. It seemed that Michael had just got off the train from Inchon. He left Inchon because he had used up all the money. Also he was very lonely.

"What happened to the money?" I asked.

No answer.

I asked again.

"*Sinbunim* will be very angry."

"No, *Sinbu* will not be angry. I just wish to know."

A slight pause. Then: "I drink, also I buy drink for friends. I drink to forget sad life."

I told him to lie down on the bed and rest awhile. Then I left to say Mass. When I returned, Michael was gone but I found a note on my desk saying that he had gone to his home in Tent City.

After breakfast I walked across town to the German Red Cross Hospital, the only hospital in Pusan for the penniless, to see if I could get Michael Rhi admitted there. It was still rather early in the morning when I arrived, but already a long line of sick people had formed before the iron gates of the hospital compound waiting for the doctor to come. Some of the people had been waiting for hours, others had been waiting for days even, sleeping at night in a corner of one of the near-by alleys. As I passed through the gates I saw one of the doctors, dressed in white, coming out of a hospital building and striding briskly along the walk toward the entrance.

I waited for him, told him what I wanted, and was politely refused. I was informed that as a matter of policy they do not treat tuberculosis cases in that hospital. They have more than they can handle, as it is, and are terribly overcrowded. In order to impress me further (I imagine the doctor saw I was none too happy at his refusal), he invited me to accompany him to the gate of the hospital and watch him make his daily selection of patients to be admitted.

I accepted the invitation. As the doctor went up and down the long line of sick people, looking each one over carefully, he explained to me the procedure. Each morning about this time, he said, he comes to the gates of the hospital and chooses the sick who are to be admitted as bed patients, the number being determined by the number of empty beds in the hospital. This morning, he told me, there were two empty beds so he could select two patients.

His criterion was very simple: the patient must be seriously ill, and there must be some possibility of recovery. If the patient is sick, but not yet on the critical list, his chances of being admitted are slim. And if the patient is so far gone that he has little hope of pulling through, he will not be accepted either. This would be just a waste of medicine and there is little medicine to waste in Korea. After a few minutes the doctor selected two patients who then moved to the front of the line. Then the doctor turned to me, shook hands, and hurried off toward the hospital.

All the way back to the bishop's house the sentence spoken to me by the mayor of Tent City kept coming to mind. "Once we're sick, we're dead."

Michael Rhi was sick, and less than six weeks after my abortive visit to the German Hospital he was dead. I learned of his death through Tallo, Michael's younger brother.

Tallo said that he had tried to see me on a number of occasions. I was sick myself at the time and each time he came he was stopped by the janitor who had taken upon himself the self-appointed task of keeping visitors away from my door, convinced that they would only disturb me. After explaining this to me, Tallo related in detail what had happened to his brother. As he spoke, his voice trembled with emotion and his eyes brimmed over with tears.

A few weeks ago, when Michael returned from Inchon to his home in Tent City, his spirit was broken and his will to live grew weaker with each passing day. It was difficult to make Michael eat anything and his mother was beside herself with anxiety and worry. The other members of the family would go without eating so that Mrs. Rhi could buy a piece of meat or fish for Michael, but even this he refused. He would just lie all day on his quilt in the corner of the room, staring at the ceiling, saying nothing.

Tallo took it upon himself on one occasion to speak very harshly to Michael in an effort to shake him up. Tallo told him if he didn't care about himself at least he should think of his mother. Look what he was doing to her! He was tormenting her, making her heart bleed, killing her! Michael said nothing, but tears began rolling down his cheeks. Tallo became silent.

Very late one night, Tallo, who slept next to Michael, woke to find Michael missing. Tallo went out looking for him and several hours later he found him. Michael was sitting on a rock near the seashore at a point on the tip of Song Do Island, about three miles from Tent City. He was just sitting there watching the movement of the water.

The night was very cold and by the time Tallo got Michael home he was practically unconscious with chills and fever. Apparently Michael had contracted pneumonia during the night, and five days later he was dead.

As his end drew near, all the bitterness and revolt seemed to drain out of him. Michael asked his mother to forgive him all the pain and sorrow he had caused her. He really didn't mean to hurt her, he just couldn't help himself. He asked Tallo and his sister Gemma, who had begun taking instructions to enter the Church, to pray the rosary for him. Also, he asked Tallo to tell me that he was sorry to learn that I was sick and he hoped that I was feeling better.

Toward the end there was much pain, but Michael didn't try to fight it. He let it come and said nothing, only groaning occasionally. It seems that he died peacefully, in his sleep.

Michael puts me in mind of a fledgling sparrow I saw in Yongdusan Park one day. A small boy had captured the sparrow and was amusing himself by torturing it. After tying a piece of string to the bird's leg, the youngster would throw it high into the air. The bird would then fly to the end of the string, flutter, beat the air wildly with its wings, and then fall back exhausted either to the ground or into his captor's hands. I took the bird from the boy despite his howling protests, broke the string, and held the bird in my hand, waiting for it to fly away. But it didn't. It just rested there in my hand, warm, fragile, and pulsating life, its eyes wide open, and a small piece of string still tied to its leg. I then set the bird on the ground amid some bushes and left it, hoping that it would regain its strength and fly away.

Michael was like this sparrow, held earthbound by a piece of string. He tried again and again, at times violently, to break away, to live, breathe, and be happy as everything within him cried out to do. But it was too much for him: finally, broken and exhausted he gave up and died.

CHAPTER NINE

❖

IT ALL BEGAN on a Sunday. After spending several hours in a cold church, hearing confessions, celebrating Mass, and administering baptism, I returned to the bishop's house chilled to the bone. I tossed and turned all night, but in the morning I felt well enough to say Mass.

At the Offertory I could feel the blood draining from my head and a cold sweat breaking out on my back. I realized then that I wasn't going to make it. I placed the chalice carefully on the corporal, then, steadying myself with both hands on the altar, breathed in slowly and deeply. My head began to reel and the next thing I knew an altar boy and the sacristan were standing over me, trying to get me on my feet. The chalice, its contents spilled on the carpet, was lying beside me on the altar platform.

I picked up the chalice, folded the corporal, put the veil on the chalice, and, with someone at each elbow to steady me, made my way back to the sacristy. I leaned upon the vesting case in the sacristy for a few minutes, until the cold clammy feeling had abated somewhat. Then I unvested. As I walked out through the church I could see concern and amazement reflected in the eyes of the attending congregation.

Back in my room I slipped into bed. A few minutes later someone came up from the kitchen with two hot water bottles. I was being broiled alive when, after a knock at the door, a dozen members of the parish burst into my room. They had just witnessed my sensational withdrawal from public life in the church and had now come to express their concern. They were most solicitous and they clucked about the room like so many mother hens, adjusting blankets, propping up pillows, pouring drinks of water, rattling off advice, and trying in general to give aid and comfort.

I was being smothered by kindness and was just getting ready to scream for help when there was another knock at the door. This time it was Sister Agnus Therese, a doctor from the Maryknoll clinic. Sister began her visit by shooing all others from the room. After an examination she gave me some medicine, promised to return in a few days, and left with the warning that I was to remain quietly in bed.

A couple of days later pain developed in the liver region and all appetite disappeared. When Sister returned after a few days she looked at me rather curiously, I thought, and after I described the newly developed symptoms she looked at me even more curiously than before. Then she brought over a mirror from the washstand, held it up before my face, and invited me to take a look. I was turning yellow.

It was a case of hepatitis, of course—and a good one. Normally, this would mean six weeks in bed and twice that long again before full recovery. I was politely instructed by the doctor to lie quietly in bed and do nothing. Not even read. Just lie there and get well. I lay there all right, but I didn't get well. Instead, various intestinal complications set in and for every step forward I would take one and a half backward.

Once you're down in Korea, it's not easy to get up. So Bishop Choi, in that time-honored yours-is-not-to-reason-why tradition of superiors, decided that I should return to the U.S. for a change of air, food, and scenery. Since I am the only American priest belonging to his diocese, the bishop further suggested that I make an effort to raise funds and find priests for Pusan during my period of convalescence in the United States.

The cost of one-way transportation to the U.S. is $500. I was without funds at the time and the coffers of the bishop's house were equally empty; but, as a result of good fortune and patient waiting, I managed to procure complimentary passage on a tramp steamer bound for Yokohama and Oakland.

Being the only passenger on the ship, I had twelve rooms, a lounge, a sun deck, and one deep and dark blue rolling ocean all to myself. The ship, empty and top-heavy, was a reconverted baby carrier. As she pitched, tossed, and rolled onward toward the Golden Gate of San Francisco, there was not much to occupy one's time. I would listen to the jukebox in the lounge, watch the gooney birds dipping and gliding about the ship, walk about on deck, read, and wonder silently if the North Pacific would not be too much for our crazy, lopsided vessel. But we made it all right.

Thirteen days after leaving Pusan, our good ship, the *Robin S. Mowbray*, docked at the pier in Oakland. As soon as the gangway was lowered, customs officials with briefcases under their arms swarmed on the ship. They set up headquarters in the lounge and began to stamp passports and inspect baggage. My turn came.

"What've you got in there, Father?" asked a smiling inspector, as he pointed to my duffel bag. "Gold or opium?"

"Both," I replied.

"Okay, you can go then."

The inspector, smiling, ruddy-complexioned, and handsome in a roly-poly way, introduced himself as Mr. Murphy and inquired about my immediate travel plans. There was a night flight at eleven forty-five from San Francisco for Washington, D.C.; I wanted to take that if possible.

"Fine," said Mr. Murphy. "If you wait another half hour I'll be glad to take you to my home. You can have supper with the family, and later on tonight I'll drive you to the airport."

My first impression upon returning to the native shores of America after my stay in Korea was one of sheer dazzlement. Pusan was still fresh in my memory. Pusan with its thousands of tents, shacks, and squatter huts, its teeming, squalid, overcrowded streets; Pusan with its beggars, refugees, orphans, ragpickers, dump-dwellers, and thousands of hungry people lining up at feeding stations each day. All this was fresh in my mind and it contrasted sharply with America, reseen and revisited after an absence.

Driving from the ship to his home, Mr. Murphy took the turnpike and we were quickly caught up in a fast-moving, silent stream of traffic, composed of a thousand shiny, expensive, built-for-speed-and-luxury cars. Mr. Murphy drove a new pink De Soto, and it blended in nicely with the current of Oldsmobiles, Fords, Plymouths, Chevies, Mercuries, and Cadillacs which flowed easily about us.

It was Sunday afternoon turning into evening, and the passengers in the cars, pleasantly worn out by a weekend at the seashore or mountains, were returning to comfortable homes. They would unpack their things, have a light buffet supper, and then settle down in an easy chair to watch Ed Sullivan on TV until it was time for bed.

We left the turnpike and drove along streets which were sweet with the smell of freshly watered lawns and budding flowers. Then we pulled into a driveway. We got out, walked across a spacious lawn, and entered a large, comfortable, upper middle-class home. The interior was cool and pleasant and was furnished with exquisite good taste.

For supper Mrs. Murphy served fried chicken, mashed potatoes, salad, asparagus, and ice cream and cake for dessert. Mr. Murphy did not take dessert: he was on a diet.

After supper we retired to the living room. The TV set was turned on and the three Murphy children stretched themselves out on the soft loam carpet and gazed up in quiet adoration at Lassie and her heart-warming adventures.

There were still another three or four hours until plane time so Mr. Murphy suggested that I call on the parish priest to pay my respects. Mr. Murphy got his pastor, whom I shall call Monsignor Smith, on the phone and mentioned that we would like to come over. The monsignor replied that he would be only too happy to see us, so come on over.

It is a ten-minute walk or a three-minute ride from Mr. Murphy's residence to the parish rectory. We rode.

As we got out of the car, Monsignor Smith was waiting at the door to meet us. He was jovial, warm, and expansive, and I liked him immediately. The visit began with a long question-and-answer period concerning conditions in Korea. This was followed by a tour of Monsignor Smith's rectory.

Spanking new and sparkling bright, $120,000 worth of rectory, it was well worth seeing. Monsignor was proud of it and he pointed out its features and highlights, with all the subdued effervescence of a soft-sell real estate agent. Central air-conditioning. Wall-to-wall carpeting. Built-in TV for each room. Adjustable lounge chairs. Indirect lighting and wood paneling throughout.

After completing our tour of the rectory, Monsignor led us to the recreation room. Standing in the middle of the room, he made a sweeping gesture to include all that we had just seen and, half-kidding, half-serious, whispered aside to me: "Take my word for it, kiddo, one day we're going to have to eat all this. Yes-sir, as sure as God made little green apples, we're going to eat every last bit of it."

Meanwhile: "What'll it be, pal?"—Monsignor was now standing in front of a cabinet containing an impressive array of bottles and glasses—"Scotch or bourbon?"

CHAPTER TEN

THE PATH OF the beggar is not always strewn with rose petals; as a matter of fact, at times it can be downright thorny. I myself traveled this path for two years during my convalescence in the United States—at first alone; then for a never-to-be-forgotten period of six months in the company of Bishop Choi.

Bishop Choi came to the United States for the usual reasons which attract native-born bishops to the shores of the Great PX. As an African bishop whom I met recently put it: "We don't come here looking for indulgences." Neither did Bishop Choi. He came primarily in search of funds and personnel for the diocese of Pusan. Immediately after Bishop Choi's arrival at Friendship Airport in Baltimore, we took to the hustings and, in the long hot months that followed, we went as far west as Minneapolis, as far north as Montreal, and as far south as Mexico City.

It was Bishop Choi's first venture outside of the rugged little peninsula which gave him life. Born of poor peasant parents in the mountain district of Kyongsang Nam Do, Bishop Choi had heard much about that shining world which lay beyond his world. Coming direct from Korea as he did and seeing it for the first time with his own eyes in all its opulence and glory, he entered a mild state of shock from which he has not yet fully recovered.

I began preparing for Bishop Choi's visit six months prior to his arrival. By the time he arrived in April, I had already set up preaching engagements in more than fifty parishes scattered throughout the United States.

Our begging efforts, at first timid and hesitant, soon fell into a fixed pattern which varied little from week to week. I would drive Bishop Choi—usually on a Friday evening—to the parish where he was scheduled to make a mission appeal on the following Sunday. After introducing him to the pastor I would leave him and then proceed to another parish where I myself was scheduled to make an appeal in Bishop Choi's name.

On Monday mornings I would rejoin Bishop Choi. During the remainder of the week we would visit American bishops and religious superiors or else give talks and slide programs in seminaries and convents in the area.

Monday morning was the brightest day in the week. I would arrive at the parish to pick up Bishop Choi and invariably I would find him bubbling over with joy. His Excellency would draw me aside to his room. Then his eyes would light up, his face break into a wide grin, and, rubbing his hands together with animation, he would exclaim: "Good success! Good success!" Then he would tell me the figure of his Sunday collection, which was always very high. His Excellency would then distractedly pull out from his pockets—like so much loose confetti—cash, checks, and assorted bits of paper on which were written names and addresses of people interested in helping him in the future. These he would give me by the fistful. I in turn would put them in my briefcase to be recorded later. Then Bishop Choi would turn to me and ask: "How did you do?" My answer was always something of a disappointment because I had the small parishes and, after all, a priest is not a bishop.

Bishop Choi himself made a good impression wherever he went. His English was rudimentary, but this didn't hurt him much. The American people respond almost instinctively to sincerity and simplicity. Bishop Choi's sincerity was at times almost painful, and his simplicity was equally engaging. So his trip—at least from a financial point of view—turned into something of a mild triumph.

Three days after his arrival in the United States, Bishop Choi preached his first sermon in the new Cathedral of Our Lady in Baltimore. This cathedral is something to see: "Not even Solomon in all his glory was arrayed like one of these." The church itself cost $13,000,000, and the rectory another million. The rectory enjoys the dubious distinction of being the costliest in the world. In defense of the plant, however, it must be stated that a certain Mr. Jenkins left $20,000,000 in his will with specific instructions that the money be used for a new cathedral—and no substitutes, please. The Baltimore archdiocese needed a new cathedral like a hole in the head. They tried but failed to break the will; and reluctant to see the money go down the drain, they decided to erect the present ecclesiastical monument.

When Bishop Choi walked into this huge edifice on Saturday afternoon and little by little it dawned on him that the next morning it would be filled with people, and that he, Bishop Choi, would be standing in the pulpit there preaching to them in English, he was not just frightened, he was terrified.

If one has seen the cathedral in Pusan, one could easily understand Bishop Choi's emotion. The cathedral in Pusan can be best compared to a large car barn with a sagging roof. And the bishop's residence in Pusan at that time (it has since been changed) was nothing to brag about either, especially when compared to the million-dollar Baltimore cathedral rectory.

The first Sunday morning Mass at the cathedral is at seven o'clock. At a quarter to seven, with the rector of the cathedral in tow, I knocked at Bishop Choi's door. I felt like an executioner who had come to call for the doomed man. There was no answer from within Bishop Choi's room. I knocked a second and a third time. Time was running out and the rector was becoming visibly impatient. I opened the door of the bishop's room and found His Excellency pacing up and down inside reading aloud his short five-minute sermon. He asked me to listen. I told him there was no time and, taking him by the sleeve, led him out to the corridor. With the cathedral rector on one side and I on the other, we walked in silence the last mile to the church sacristy. Actually, Bishop Choi's fears were groundless: his appeal was well received and went straight to the hearts—and pocketbooks—of his listeners.

After the last Mass on Sunday, Bishop Choi insisted on having his photograph taken in front of the cathedral, then in the pulpit, and next in front of the rectory. He was afraid that if he told the people back home about it they would think he was only dreaming, and so he wanted photographs as visual proof.

Bishop Choi's visit to Cardinal Cushing was also something to remember and write home about. When I called up to make the appointment, who should answer the phone but His Eminence himself. I had met him before and recognized immediately the gruff, sandpaper voice which growled: "Wadda ya want?" I arranged the appointment and Bishop Choi and I were waiting in the cardinal's study at 2 P.M. on the assigned day. Shortly after two, the doors of the elevator swung open and out came His Eminence. He had obviously been napping, and, rubbing the sleep out of his eyes and buttoning up his cassock, he waved to the bishop and said: "Hi ya, Bishop!" I was waiting for the bishop to reply with a "Hi ya, Cardinal!" but I was disappointed. Instead, Bishop Choi knelt down and kissed the cardinal's ring. After listening to what the bishop had to say about Korea, the cardinal delivered himself of some thoughts concerning the Church in South America. He talked at some length about "those bishops down there in their ivory towers, and the Church identified with the rich. What they need is a social revolution. I got a mind to lead it myself." Then the cardinal paused and, turning to me, he said in a low voice behind the back of his hand: "Better not tell your bishop what I'm saying. He'll think I'm a damned radical."

After promising Bishop Choi financial help, Cardinal Cushing ended the interview and we left. Bishop Choi had met a man as simple and sincere as himself, and he was impressed. Of all the prelates in the U.S., Cardinal Cushing made the strongest impression upon Bishop Choi. This, of course, will come as no surprise to those who are familiar with the inimitable warmth and style of the cardinal archbishop of Boston.

Most American bishops—like Cardinal Cushing—received Bishop Choi cordially and were genuinely interested in what he had to say. There were of course exceptions, and one especially comes to mind. We had made an appointment with a bishop in the Midwest. After waiting for two or three hours, the bishop not only did not show up for the appointment, but did not even trouble himself to offer an excuse or an explanation. Bishop Choi was understandably upset and, after getting in our car, he pulled out of his coat pocket a small package of cigarettes which had been given him by the airlines on the flight from Korea. Although he and I are both non-smokers, Bishop Choi took a cigarette, then offered me one with the words: "Let's smoke. When I'm angry and I light a cigarette," he explained, "the anger sometimes goes up in smoke." This idea interested me, so after finishing our cigarettes I turned to Bishop Choi and asked: "Feel any better now?" He answered: "No. Let's say the rosary." After the rosary he announced that he felt better.

Unless the person addressing Bishop Choi spoke clearly and slowly, the bishop had a hard time following what was being said. This proved no handicap, for His Excellency possessed a flair for acting plus the ability to mirror perfectly the expression of the one speaking to him, so it would come about that the person speaking would be convinced that Bishop Choi grasped fully all the conversation that flowed in his direction. This, however, was usually not the case.

One example comes to mind. A bishop in the Midwest was driving Bishop Choi and myself around his diocese showing us various points of interest. The American bishop kept up a merciless stream of puns and jokes. He pointed to the bugs on the window shield and said: "What did the bug say when he hit the window shield?" Blank silence from Bishop Choi. The American bishop answered. "It takes guts to stick to this thing! Ha! Ha! Ha!" Although he did not understand, Bishop

Choi would come in on cue and join in the laughter. Encouraged, the American bishop continued: "What did another bug say when he hit the window shield?" "That's me all over! Ha! Ha! Ha!" And again Bishop Choi would valiantly "Ha! Ha! Ha!" in return, and everybody was happy. Later, when alone, Bishop Choi asked me to explain the meaning of these jokes, but I'm afraid they were just a bit too much for the Oriental mind.

Bishop Choi was not much on protocol, and I was something less than an authority myself. One dignified bishop in Mexico whom we were visiting was appalled by our antics. Calling me aside, the bishop gave me a brief lecture in episcopal protocol. Among other interesting items I learned that the protocol position in an automobile is the right-hand corner. I, as the bishop's assistant, was to open the door, let the bishop enter and sit in the right-hand corner, close the door, then scoot around to the other side and get in beside the bishop. This, of course, was, when I was not chauffeuring the car myself. With my instructor, the Mexican bishop, looking on, I opened the back door of the car, and Bishop Choi got in. I closed the door and by the time I got around to the other side Bishop Choi had already scooted across the back seat of the car—as I knew would happen—and was happily ensconced in the non-protocol position. A smiling Bishop Choi motioned me to get in on the other side and occupy what was supposed to be the protocol seat. Shrugging my shoulders at the nonplussed Mexican bishop, I dutifully obeyed.

Occasionally Bishop Choi's English pronunciation would get him into trouble. For instance, we were in Toronto, Canada, visiting the new $6,000,000 Motherhouse of the Sisters of Saint Joseph. It is a glass and marble wonder with electronic doors which swing open automatically as you enter. As the Mother General showed us around, Bishop Choi kept exclaiming: "Too good! Too good!" In Korean, "too good!" —*nomu chosumnida*—is a superlative form of praise, meaning "extremely good." The Mother General, however, took it as a reproach, and she objected: "No, Bishop, it's not *too* good." At this, Bishop Choi replied with more animation than before, "Yes, yes, too good! too good!" I tried to explain to His Excellency the meaning of "too good!" but he liked the expression and was not to part with it easily. Unfortunately, however, nearly everything he saw in the States was "too good! too good!"

After our visit and talk at the Motherhouse in Toronto, the Mother General and her dignified assistants gathered around the bishop for punch and cookies. It was a pleasant social gathering and the Sisters were all smiling sweetly. Bishop Choi, noticing the Sisters' smiling, remarked with much feeling: "I am always so happy to meet Sisters who smell." Upon hearing this, the Sisters' expressions froze. I interjected softly, "His Excellency means 'smile.'" The bishop, listening to me, added: "Yes, that's what I said, smell, smell."

Traveling as I did with Bishop Choi, I myself had occasion to see America fresh through the eyes of a Korean national. It was quite an experience—enlightening as well as amusing. For instance, the first time that Bishop Choi ate in an American restaurant (actually a roadside lunchroom), I ordered grilled-cheese sandwiches, Cokes, and vanilla ice cream. After serving us, the waitress returned and placed the check face down on the counter in front of Bishop Choi. Before I could make a move, His Excellency had reached for it and when his eyes fell upon the figure $1.20 at the bottom they flew wide open in sheer disbelief. One dollar and twenty cents just for lunch? That's more than a laborer earns in Korea in a day! At this juncture I had the temerity, rashness, foolhardiness to place a quarter tip on the counter—in Korea one does not tip— and then proceed to walk away from it. Bishop Choi spotted the shiny piece of silver which I had detached from my possessions (our possessions), and an explanation was called for.

After this initial experience, lunch while traveling usually consisted of sandwiches (peanut butter, baloney, or cheese) which were prepared in the morning, and Cokes which were purchased cold from a Coke machine at the nearest gas station. On another occasion we were en route to Rochester, New York. We had stopped for lunch in the beautiful, sparkling, fresh green mountains of upstate Pennsylvania. After eating, I picked up a Coke bottle, the contents of which I had just drained, threw it high into the air, then watched it descend into an empty pasture below. As the bottle hit the ground and began rolling down the grassy slope, Bishop Choi smilingly remarked, "Next time throw it as far as Korea. There the beggars would fight each other to gain possession of it."

Then there was the time we were passing through Wilmington, Delaware. With that raw curiosity which one encounters only in the Orient, Bishop Choi was staring hard at an old Negro junk dealer who was pushing a baby carriage piled high with papers, rags, and scrap metal over the broken pavement alongside our car. His eyes still riveted on the ragpicker, Bishop Choi said, "Look, a poor man, just like in Korea. Still I am surprised. He looks well fed. How does he get food to eat?" I explained that he probably gets enough to eat from the results of his work or perhaps from some welfare agency. For the first time Bishop Choi averted his gaze from the junk dealer, looked at me, and said, "Oh, he's not poor then. If he has food to eat, he can hardly be considered poor."

After visiting some of our large cities in the United States, Bishop Choi felt that they all resembled ghost towns. "Where is everybody at?" he would exclaim. In Korea everybody is outdoors, the streets are always crowded and teeming with people, and at night one wonders how they all manage to fit inside. In America everyone is at home, at work, or traveling about by car or some other mode of transportation.

Bishop Choi was also very impressed by the parks he encountered in American cities—not by their size, their number, or their beauty, but by something else completely different. What impressed him most about these parks was the fact that dead branches were allowed to collect naturally on the ground, untouched and unmolested by people. In Korea people walk miles and miles into the mountains in search of such treasure as loose firewood—and here in America no one looks twice at it. Truly, this is a marvelous country!

When we came upon our first automobile cemetery, Bishop Choi was again struck by the wonder and marvel of life in America. The fact that such wealth as automobiles, albeit used and battered ones, could be discarded in such callous and offhanded fashion taxed his power of belief to the breaking point. "Why, if this were Korea. . . ."

One day in the Midwest, being without a box lunch, Bishop Choi and I stopped at a McDonald's Drive-In for hamburgers. I had opened my hamburger and was just squirting it generously with mustard. Bishop Choi looked at it for a moment, then remarked, "Enjoy it. That's more meat than my brothers and sisters will see for a whole year."

Returning to home base in Washington, D.C., after several weeks on the road, we found the house empty. My father and sisters were away on vacation. As suppertime approached, I suggested that we go out for dinner since there was no one at home to prepare a good meal. Bishop Choi smiled disarmingly and said, "How can I spend money in a restaurant knowing at the same time that my people in Korea are hungry. Let's get some milk out of the icebox and some bread out of the pantry and be satisfied with that for supper." Which we did, for the first night at least. After that I began serving the bishop the very best of Morton's TV dinners, ready to eat and piping hot out of the kitchen oven.

At home, Bishop Choi was a delightful guest, much easier to please than the simplest layman. One evening, since my sister was out and my father does not like TV dinners, I fixed some steaks. After dinner, Bishop Choi, my father, and I were all in the parlor watching TV, but Bishop Choi looked worried. Finally turning to my father he asked: "Who is going to clean up the dishes?" My father replied jokingly: "Why, you are, Your Excellency. It's your turn you know." At this, Bishop Choi got up, took off coat and collar, and went into the kitchen. From the kitchen came sounds of running water and various crashing sounds of pots, pans, and dishes being banged around. Finally I went into the kitchen and tried to explain to Bishop Choi that my father—in that time-honored American tradition—was pulling his leg. But the bishop was in a determined mood and it took some doing to separate His Excellency from the pots and pans and to get him back into the parlor.

Then there was the time in Albany when we stayed overnight at the Chancery Building and were invited to dine with the monsignori who lived and worked there. As supper got under way it was evident that no mercy was to be shown us. A maid placed steaks in front of Bishop Choi and me, the size of which would make a lumberjack groan inwardly with anticipated agony. I managed to eat a quarter of my steak, then laid down knife and fork in quiet surrender. But Bishop Choi was made of stronger stuff and he struggled onward until there was not a bit of steak left on his plate. He was sick for two days afterward; but finish it he did. Later, when asked why he did not leave the steak when he realized it was too much for him, Bishop Choi replied with a Korean expression which I was to hear often in the months that followed: "*Akkapta.*" It is only one word but it contains a wealth of meaning. It can be translated as: "It is too good and valuable to waste."

When Bishop Choi first arrived in the States he was wearing a curious pair of high-heeled black shoes. I could not imagine where he got them and was reluctant to ask. One day, however, because of the awkward high heel Bishop Choi sprained his ankle and, not being able to hold it in any longer, I finally asked him where in the world did he got those strange-looking shoes. "Oh," he replied, "the Maryknoll Sisters in Pusan gave them to me." So the mystery was solved: they were nun's shoes, no less. After the bishop's accident, try as I did I could not persuade him to buy a new pair of shoes. Instead, he compromised by having the heels of the old ones cut in half.

They still looked a bit odd, but at least they were no longer hazardous.

Bishop Choi's eyesight was poor, and although he wore glasses they didn't seem to help much. One day I asked where he bought the glasses. "I got them in the Pusan market," he said. "They cost fifty cents." And no wonder; after examining them I saw that the lenses were not much stronger than windowpane glass.

Shortly before the bishop was scheduled to leave the United States, he had an appointment with a prelate in Michigan. At the time, Bishop Choi needed a haircut badly. Before the meeting, then, I suggested that he visit a barber shop. "No," Bishop Choi protested, "in three weeks I will be in Europe; and in Europe haircuts are cheaper than in the United States. I will wait until then." How he found out that haircuts were cheaper in Europe than in the United States I do not know; after a while, however, I came to suspect that this type of knowledge was mystically infused, rather than acquired.

When Bishop Choi first arrived in the United States, I met him at the airport in my shiny black Renault-Dauphine. During the ride from the airport to the city I explained to His Excellency how economical the car was, but at the same time expressed doubt as to its suitability for chauffeuring the episcopacy. Between bishop and Renault, however, it was love at first sight. Bishop Choi's only point of comparison was one battered Korean jeep and he felt that in a Renault he would be traveling in great style. So instead of purchasing a Ford or a Chevy, as I was thinking of doing, I remained faithful to the Dauphine. As a result, we had several delightful adventures and misadventures.

For example, on a sunny Sunday afternoon in Baltimore a group of wealthy and influential Catholics were giving a cocktail party in Bishop Choi's honor. We arrived early, in a plush section of Baltimore, parked our car before the deluxe residence where the affair was to be held, and went inside.

Just as the guests were beginning to file in, the host called me aside and led me out to the front steps where a police officer was waiting. He informed me that the policeman had been sent by headquarters to handle traffic for the cocktail hour. Then the police officer, brimming over with zeal and good will, mentioned that he had decided to call the traffic department and request a tow truck to remove the cars in front of the house. If we do that, you see, when the bishop's limousine pulls up he can park right in front and he won't have to walk so far to get into the house. Waddya think, Father? I explained that the bishop's limousine had already arrived and, as a matter of fact, there she is. I pointed to the little black Renault glistening in the afternoon sun. The host was visibly shaken by this revelation.

The policeman, however, reacted nobly and, without breaking stride, he said, "I'm an Episcopalian, Father, and if some of our la-di-da bishops would travel like that instead of cruising about in their Caddies and Continentals our church would be a lot better off." To which I said, "Amen" and we all went inside for cocktails.

In a talk to a group of nuns in Washington just before he departed, Bishop Choi expressed some of his thoughts concerning the Church in America.

"I am a little bishop from a little country," he said. "What is more, I am a foreigner and a stranger. America is a big and powerful nation and when I first came here I was afraid that I would not be treated well. Wherever I went, however, I was not treated as a little bishop from a little country, nor as a foreigner and a stranger. I was treated as a bishop of the Catholic Church. Everywhere—in convents, rectories, and homes of individual Catholics—I was received with the same respect and reverence that Americans show their own bishops. Truly this is a sign of the deep faith of American Catholics in the universality of the Church and I myself was most impressed by it.

"I was also overjoyed to discover the astounding vitality and dynamism of the Catholic Church in America. Everywhere I went I saw new schools, convents, rectories, and institutions, all being erected under Catholic auspices. It is no exaggeration to state that at present the Church in America is the strongest in the world.

"And the generosity of American Catholics, this, too, was a constant source of amazement for me. As soon as I would tell the Catholics of our needs in Korea they would be ready, willing, and even anxious to give and to sacrifice. Even little Catholic children, sometimes they would come to the sacristy after Mass and give me all the money they had in their pockets.

"Certainly the Catholics in America have a right to be proud of their country. The land is good and sweet, and nothing is lacking here. You have been marvelously blessed by God both spiritually and materially."

Now was the hour when we were to say good-by. After six months in the States it was time for Bishop Choi to leave. It was arranged that he would go unaccompanied to Europe and I would join him in a few weeks. He had bought a ticket on a tourist flight to Rome. In the morning when we weighed Bishop Choi's baggage we discovered that it was twelve pounds over the forty-four-pound limit. The overweight penalty is two dollars per pound, and Bishop Choi worried about this all day as we rushed madly about New York on last-minute errands. (To make matters worse that day, I got a fifteen-dollar parking ticket. I did not have the heart to tell Bishop Choi, so I simply said that the suspicious-looking piece of cardboard tucked under the windshield wiper was merely an invitation to contribute to the City Welfare Fund.)

Anyway, we arrived at Idlewild Airport a little late and went directly to the Alitalia ticket counter. I left Bishop Choi waiting in line with his baggage while I hurried upstairs to make an urgent phone call. I was delayed and, when I returned, the bishop—ticket, baggage, and all—had already been checked in. I asked the bishop how much he had to pay for excess baggage. He flashed his victory smile and said, "Nothing,

nothing at all. As a matter of fact, my baggage was a few ounces below the limit." I looked at the bishop more closely and the more I looked the wider grew my smile until it required a real effort on my part to keep from laughing outright. What His Excellency had done was to remove his winter overcoat and another topcoat from his baggage and put these on over two suitcoats. Then he had filled up all his pockets with loose paraphernalia taken from the suitcases. It was a sweltering, mid-September evening in New York, but the bishop looked very relaxed. After all, he had just economized twenty dollars, which is more than enough to pay a catechist's salary in Korea for a whole month. This knowledge soothed the inner man and brought cool comfort to his soul. As he lumbered up the gangway to board the plane, however, Bishop Choi looked more like an astronaut heading for outer space than a prelate en route to Rome.

CHAPTER ELEVEN

ONE MONTH AFTER Bishop Choi's departure from the United States I met him in Paris as planned. We spent three weeks together on the European begging circuit; then we flew over the Pole back to Korea.

We arrived in Pusan in time to celebrate Christmas. On Christmas morning Bishop Choi offered Mass at the cathedral and delivered a sermon to a crowded congregation. During his sermon, Bishop Choi was so overcome with emotion at the thought of his successful trip and his subsequent safe return to Pusan that he gave way to tears. Many members of the congregation, catching his emotion, broke down and cried also.

Many changes had taken place in Korea since my trip to America. For one thing, there had been a change in government. A military junta seized power in a bloodless coup in the spring of 1961. This junta, since legitimatized by national elections, is still riding herd on the country today, and doing it more or less effectively. Some of the graft, corruption, and "saba saba" which plagued Korea in the past seems to have been partially eliminated. The streets of the cities have also been cleaned up to some extent. In general there seems to be more order, discipline, and building activity in the country.

One suspects, however, that Korea's sudden-blooming prosperity does not go far below the surface. Underneath, Korea is still Korea and the living here is still anything but easy.

One example, taken from the common everyday, man-in-the-street level, will help to illustrate my point. Juliana Kim is a fervent member of the Legion of Mary in the parish where I am now stationed. Juliana was living with her father, mother, two brothers, and a sister in a one-room shack on the slope of a mountain just opposite the church. Juliana and her family were not just poor, they were destitute; and when her father died recently they found they had no money to bury him. A few hours after her father's death, Juliana herself went to the Pusan University Hospital to sell her blood in order to get money for the funeral. It does not take much to bury one in Korea. A wooden coffin, clean clothes, and a small plot of ground are all that is needed; in all, about seven or eight dollars. Juliana received three dollars for her blood, which left her four dollars short. Two of her fellow Legion members came to see me and asked if I couldn't do something to help. I could and, of course, I did. Juliana herself, her face drawn and eyes red from lack of sleep, came shortly afterward to thank me.

Chairman Park Chunghee has drawn up a Five Year Plan for Korea with hopes of increasing the gross national product by forty per cent. It is a little like reaching for the moon; but even if General Park were to succeed in achieving his goal, Korea's rapid population growth (three per cent a year) will have all but canceled out its economic advance. The point is that, although Korea has come a long way in the past few years, she still has a long road to travel before achieving ultimate economic stability and independence.

The people in the parish where I am living are the poorest of the poor. Many are refugees from North Korea. Most of them live from day to day and from hand to mouth. Except for forty families who dwell in a Catholic housing project near the church, the majority of the people live in shacks and hovels built on top of each other in closely packed, air-tight clusters.

Summoned to anoint a dying woman recently I had occasion to visit a hovel more or less typical of the dwellings in this area. The old woman was lying on the floor in a corner of a room about the size of an average American bathroom. The ceiling was very low and one could not stand upright without striking his head. The old woman shared the room with her son, daughter-in-law, two grandchildren, and a small army of flies. There was a minuscule annex attached to the room which served as kitchen, and this constituted the total living space for this family of five. I anointed the woman, spoke a few words of encouragement, and left.

On the way back to the church I discovered that I was in a somber mood and had no trouble at all thinking some bitter thoughts. Among other things I thought of dogs. Not that I have anything against dogs, but I thought how last year in America more than a billion dollars was spent on food to nourish them. I also thought of their living quarters, the weatherproof kennels in which they dwell, the yards and open space in which they can romp and play, and the medical treatment which they often receive when sick. I thought of all this and came to the conclusion that the average dog in America has a considerably higher standard of living than the average member of my parish here in Korea. Is this the order God intended for his world, or do the children of the poor have a right to expect something better?

My thinking was interrupted by the ear-shattering shrieks of a small band of children who had spotted me from behind the church and were racing up the hill to meet me. (I have always maintained that, pound for pound and inch for inch, the kids in my parish have the strongest lung power this side of the Thirty-eighth Parallel.) In an instant the children—dirty-faced, runny-nosed, and ragtailed—were all over me, shouting and fighting for my hand. I have been told by members of the parish that the children are far too undisciplined and should be taught to respect me more. I agree, and what is more, someday I plan to do something about it.

My progress, already made difficult by the youngsters clinging to me, was stopped altogether when one little four-year-old locked his arms around my legs and held on with the tenacity of a four-year-old bulldog. I looked down at him menacingly and he looked back at me with his big brown eyes. It was a test of wills. Finally he said: *"Uri sinbunim. Uri sinbunim."* (Our Spiritual Father.)

This cut right through me, and, disentangling myself from him and the rest of the band, I hurried inside the rectory. I fixed a cup of coffee, sat down at the kitchen table, and the words of St. Vincent de Paul came to mind. He was chaplain of the French Royal Court at the time and in the atmosphere of luxury and ease in which he was forced to live he felt something inside of him beginning to suffocate. He decided once and for all to leave the court and go back to his poor. The queen tried to retain him, but he silenced her with one emotionally charged sentence. He said: *"J'ai besoin de mes pauvres."* (I have need of my poor.)

A missioner, too, has need of his poor. Just how much, I myself never realized until being allowed to return to Korea.

During the weeks immediately after my return to Korea I took long walks through Pusan in order to rediscover the physiognomy of my city. It is difficult to express in a single phrase or sentence what Pusan is really like. It is not one dish—but rather a potpourri or smorgasbord of life. The following items—pulled out from memory without too much thought to logic or order—will perhaps give the reader a sharper idea of what Pusan looks like, sounds like, and smells like.

Pusan Street Scenes: High school boys, silhouetted against an early morning sky, stand on the ridge of a mountain near Pusan and shout, sing, and yell in an effort to strengthen voice and vocal chords. One day they will be great lawyers, singers, politicians, teachers. . . .

Boys with close-cropped black hair, dressed in the black cotton trousers and jacket of the student, walk arm in arm down the road leading to the park, singing *"Qué será, será,* whatever will be, will be." This song is a favorite with students because of its plaintive melody and fatalistic message. . . .

Businessmen with sharp, crafty eyes sit at low tables in the teahouses, discussing in low voices weighty matters concerning contracts, propositions, and deals. Worldly looking, Western-clad hostesses glide about, bringing them tea and whisky. . . .

Schoolgirls in blue cotton trousers, white blouses, and blue jackets, their black hair cut short in a straight bob, walk together to school, singing. Everyone in Korea sings, voices true and on pitch. They are called the "Welsh of the Far East." . . .

In the streets passersby stop to look at gaudy, brightly colored display cards in theater windows, advertising the next American movie. *Bus Stop*, with Marilyn Monroe, comes to town next week. A hundred won* will purchase an admission ticket and will provide escape into a Hollywood dream world of long cars, fine clothes, and rich living. . . .

In the park, women with white bandannas tied tightly about their heads, their faces tough, leathery, and weather-worn, offer a popgun or a bow and arrow to people strolling by. Only ten won, and if you hit the bull's-eye of the target you win a small box of candy. They carry their children on their backs and when these begin to cry they swing them around front and nurse them at the breast. . . .

A storyteller in the parks holds sway over a rapt audience composed mostly of old men. These latter are clothed in white, wear quaint, lacquered, horsehair hats, and smoke long-stemmed pipes. On the fringe of this group moves an excited, fidgety, mischievous band of children. . . .

A patent-medicine seller beats a drum with his feet and at the same time plays a violin with his hands, while a large crowd forms a circle about him. A blind boy plays a flute with his nose to the amusement of another crowd of people. The streets of Korea are filled with people who have nothing

* The unit of currency in Korea was changed in 1962 from hwan to won. At present one dollar equals 270 won.

to do, people looking for bread to satisfy them or circuses to distract them. Create the slightest disturbance and immediately a large, curious, escape-hungry crowd forms about you. . . .

On the street corners men stand idle with jiggey frames on their backs, pocketed hands and drooping heads, waiting to be hired. For every job to be filled there are three men to apply. . . .

Early Sunday morning, en route to the church on Yongdo Island, I pass a procession of women moving slowly across the bridge on their way to market. Huge bundles are balanced on their heads and scarves are pulled tightly across their faces to protect them from the wind. They work seven days a week, sunup to sundown, trying to sell articles of merchandise in order to earn a few won. "Yesterday I sold nothing, perhaps someone will buy from me today. . . ."

Men and boys in pajamas emerge at dawn from their huts and begin splashing themselves from a basin of cold water. Women come out later to empty the night vases along the side of the road. . . .

Women divers with large baskets strapped on their backs go to the seashore in the early afternoon. The water is cold but the divers are tough, the toughest of the tough. They dive in December as well as in May. Later they return to the city, the baskets now dripping with a heavy load of seaweed. The seaweed is sold on the market and soup is made from it. . . .

Korean New Year dancers in gaudy costumes beat drums and tambourines, laugh and cavort to the amusement of many. They are rewarded with glasses of rice wine. Their faces are flushed and their eyes are glazed with liquid happiness. . . .

Small girls propel each other four or five feet into space by jumping up and down on a piece of board placed on a fulcrum made from a mound of earth. Two girls stretch a long rubber cord between them, while two other girls sing, dance, turn, and twist about it. One little girl plays jump rope with her little brother tied on her back. They have amazing spring in their legs and they play at these jumping games with an abundance of natural grace and ease. . . .

Sitting in the sun on the park bench, I am disturbed by three children who take up positions directly in front of me and stare, and stare, and stare. I look at them and they look back at me full in the face, through dark, silent, completely unself-conscious eyes. They are held spellbound by my Western nose and hazel-colored eyes. How is it possible for anyone to see out of eyes that are not black or dark brown? . . .

A girl in tight, ill-fitting Western skirt and jacket, balanced precariously on high-heeled shoes, struts through the streets of Pusan. She is followed by a band of staring, disbelieving children who are cowed into silence by such a startling sight. . . .

It has been said, by a Western observer in Korea, that the Korean just naturally gravitates away from danger, while the westerner will gravitate toward it. Proof: One evening I am walking through the streets of Pusan with two Korean priests, one on my left side and one on my right, when suddenly the sidewalk falls from under me and I find myself in an open sewer up to my waist. The two Korean priests laughingly pull me out and shake their heads in wonder. A Korean would never falls into such a hole, although it is open and unmarked. . . .

A careening bus knocks a youth from his bicycle and sends him flying head over tin cup into a near-by ditch. The young man staggers to his feet, brushes himself off, and, laughing happily, gets back on his bicycle and pedals away. . . .

A farmer carefully pedals his bicycle through the perilous traffic of downtown Pusan, with a large pig tied on the back. His front wheel gets caught in a streetcar track. The farmer goes sprawling and his pig breaks loose. The pig races down the street and the farmer takes off after him, shouting and gesticulating. . . .

While waiting for a red light to change, a driver of a jeep rests his arm on the windowsill of his vehicle. A thief spots an elastic band wristwatch on the man's arm, slips it off, and dashes away. The driver flings open the door of the jeep and takes off in hot pursuit. Another thief, who had been watching the action from the sidelines, jumps in the driver seat of the jeep and pulls away. The driver stops in his tracks and watches helplessly as his jeep goes in one direction, his wristwatch in another. . . .

Blind fortune-tellers sit all day in their kennel-like lean-to's under the bridge, waiting for a customer who is willing to invest a few won to learn the hidden secrets of the future. . . .

"Home, Sweet Home" is written with mud in large English letters on the side of a dilapidated tent dwelling which I recently passed.

A beggar sleeps in an alleyway using straw as a mattress and a piece of cardboard as a blanket; bare feet protrude revealing frostbitten toes. . . . Three small boys lie on the sidewalk with a thin blanket thrown over them, huddled together like puppies to keep warm. . . . A man with no legs is nearly run over as he slides across a busy street on his rear end. . . . A woman lies on the pavement, face contorted by pain, clutching her stomach as three runny-nosed children cling bewilderedly to her skirts. . . . Children sidle up to well-dressed people on the streets and cling to them like parasites until they extort the pittance which they consider their due. . . . A woman sits on the street corner in front of the bank, laughing hysterically for hours. . . . Mothers do the family wash in the gutters, using the dirty water which flows from the public bathhouse. . . . Merchants stolidly stand from morning till night beside stalls which contain twenty or thirty old copies of *Time* and *Life*, or a few flashlights, or some canned goods stolen from the Army PX. . . . Old women patiently squat beside small mounds of tobacco garnered from discarded cigarette butts found in the gutters, trying to earn a few won.

Pusan Street Sounds: The endless bleating and honking of car horns as the taxi drivers drive with one foot on the accelerator and one hand on the klaxon. . . . The click-click of the huge tin scissors used to announce the coming of the candy seller. . . . The thud of the muffled drum which the lotion merchant employs to attract attention. . . . The dull sound of the night watchman's wooden clack as he makes his rounds through Pusan's meandering streets, on the alert for fires or burglars. . . . Students singing Western pop songs from five o'clock in the morning until the night curfew at twelve o'clock. . . . The older people singing melancholy Korean folk songs with plaintive melodies. . . . Children laughing and shouting at play in the streets. . . . Loud music blaring from record shops in the streets below. . . . The militant music of the Salvation Army band in the park inviting all to repentance and salvation. . . . The chimes from a near-by Presbyterian Church playing "Auld Lang Syne" every night at ten.

Pusan Street Smells: Kamgae muryang. (Beyond the power of description.)

CHAPTER TWELVE

IT WAS A RAW, chilly evening, and the rain outside was coming down in sheets. I thought I heard someone at the front door, but I wasn't sure. Then it came again, this time unmistakable, a timid tap-tap-tapping on the glass panel of the front entrance. I opened the door to admit a young man who could easily have passed for fourteen, but who I later learned was nineteen. His black cotton jeans and brown threadbare corduroy shirt were soaked through. He removed his cap and began twisting it about in his hands as he sought words to explain his presence. Very thin, deathly pale, and not just frightened but terrified, he was a pathetic figure.

"*Sinbunim imnikka?*" he began. Yes, I answered, I was the Spiritual Father.

"My name is I Khi Young," he said. "I am a pagan, but I wish to talk to a priest. I wish to confess my sins. All the bad and stupid things I have done in my life I wish to tell you. I want God's forgiveness. There is not much time."

Sigani opsumnida. The long conversation which followed was constantly punctuated by this short, at first enigmatic, phrase: "There is not much time."

I showed the youth into my room, offered him a chair, and slipped into the kitchen. I came out with a tray containing bread, butter, and coffee which I placed in front of him. When he got up to go an hour later, the food and beverage had not been touched.

I sat down in a chair opposite him and told him that if he wanted to talk, go ahead; I would listen.

He wanted to talk all right, but he didn't know where to begin. Rubbing the finger of one hand up and down against the bridge of his nose and wetting his lips with his tongue, he searched for a beginning. Once started, however, his words poured out in cascade; so much so that several times I had to ask him to speak more slowly so that I could understand better what he was saying.

One thing which I could understand clearly, however, was that one, ever-recurring, mysterious phrase: *Sigani opsumnida.* There is not much time.

At one point Khi Young asked in a small, pleading voice if I could forgive his sins in God's name. I told him that although Catholics could receive the sacrament of confession, it was not the Church's practice to administer it to the non-baptized. This information in no way deterred him. He still wanted to tell someone whom he considered God's representative all about his life and "bad actions."

His life? A pattern of poverty, loneliness, and family tragedy. His mother had died when he was six. His father had married again, but his stepmother turned out to be a real shrew. Family life soon degenerated into an unending torrent of abuse heaped on his father for failing to earn more money. His father took to drink and finally ended it all by drowning himself in the waters of Pusan Bay. Khi Young was in the seventh grade at the time of his father's death. After this family tragedy, however, all thoughts of further schooling were put aside and Khi Young was turned out on the streets of Pusan to earn money. Shoe-shine boy, hotel drummer, candy merchant, newspaper boy, petty thief, and pickpocket, he had tried everything. Many times there was nothing to eat in the house.

"Do you know what it is, *Sinbunim,*" he asked, "to come home to a house in which there is no food? Not even a grain of rice. Nothing at all. Do you know what it is?" There was a note of terror in his voice.

I thought for a moment. No, I guess I didn't know what it was. But, hearing him say it with that tone in his voice and that look in his eye, I could imagine a little what it would be like.

Before sending him out of the house in the morning, his stepmother would make him promise to bring home a hundred hwan before nightfall. "Don't you come back here," she would scream, "unless you have a hundred hwan to give me." Afraid of a beating or a tongue-lashing, very often Khi Young would not come home. Instead, he slept at nights in alleyways and under bridges; in winter at times standing up in a telephone booth.

Finally his stepmother found another man, sold their shack, and went to live with her new husband. There was no room for Khi Young, his older sister, and his younger brother. His brother went to live with distant cousins; his sister took up living quarters with a young man whom she had met; and Khi Young took to the streets. For a while he worked in a shipbuilding factory, for a while he lived with a community of ragpickers. But mostly he was alone, by himself, one against the world. And this hurt more than anything else; more than the hunger, the hardship, and the poverty. Much more.

And the "bad actions?" Really not much. A series of thefts, fights, and deceptions most of which were related to the fundamental problem of staying alive and finding food for one's belly.

I Khi Young was possessed by a driving passion to study. He dreamed of becoming a writer. He spent much of his free time in the public library, devouring whatever work of literature he could get his hands on. He was almost pathologically jealous of boys of his age who had the opportunity to go to school. He would pick fights with them as they came home from school and release pent-up frustration in flailing arms and thrashing fists. Small and slightly built, he usually got the worst end of the bargain, but this did not deter him.

Now he was weary of it all; he couldn't take any more; he had had enough. And so he had made his decision: he would end it all by suicide, as his father had done. Just before knocking at the rectory door he had swallowed a bottle of poison tablets which he had been carrying around in his pocket for a month. "Since I am dying now, *Sinbunim*, and there is no time, will you give me baptism? Please? *Sigani opsumnida.*

At first, I wondered if I had heard right. Guessing my incredulity, Khi Young quickly took out of his pocket a small brown empty medicine bottle and held it out for me to take. I saw that not only the hand which held the bottle, but his whole body as well, was trembling like a leaf. I read the label: "Atabrine—Not to be taken without prescription of physician." How many tablets had he taken? The whole bottle. Maybe twenty-five, maybe thirty. He did not know for sure.

I got one of the Maryknoll doctors on the telephone and asked if she knew anything about Atabrine. "Oh yes, Father," came the matter-of-fact reply, "that's what they take. Offhand I can't tell you the exact toxicity of Atabrine, but it's dangerous all right."

When he saw me pick up the telephone, Khi Young started to bolt for the door, but I motioned to him sharply to remain where he was and he had obeyed. Now, I took Khi Young into the sacristy of the church, baptized him, then sent him to the hospital with the catechist.

At the hospital they put a stomach pump in him and a few days later he was back at the rectory, looking a little weak and shaky, but apparently none the worse for wear. I had a small room in the rectory which was not being used at the time, so I told Khi Young that if he liked he was welcome to come and live with me. He accepted gratefully.

The first evening at the rectory, out of a clear blue sky, Khi Young asked: "Father, can I ever become a real person?"

The question caught me by surprise. I glanced at the one asking, and in Khi Young's bright dark eyes there burned an anguish so intense that at first I knew neither how nor what to answer.

"Why, sure," I found myself saying, "sure you can. In no time at all, after you get some good food, rest, and a little peace you won't be able to recognize yourself."

The question, however, was so lucid and revealing that it hurt. There was still something so wild, untamed, and sensitive in Khi Young's manner that he reminded one more of some woodland animal than a city boy of nineteen. He made me think of a young doe which I had seen on a visit to Father Kim's parish in Masan. One of Father's parishioners captured the animal in the mountains a few days before and had presented it to Father Kim as a gift. It was a delicate, fragile, beautiful thing, with dark, bright, sad eyes; terribly high-strung, sensitive, and with nervous energy, like so much high-tension voltage, flitting back and forth just below the surface. This was I Khi Young: Pusan's answer to Hollywood's James Dean, minus the sham, artifice, and sophistication of the latter.

One morning after breakfast Khi Young came to my room carrying in his arms a stack of fifteen or twenty notebooks. They were poems and diaries, he explained, which he had written during the last five or six years. Now he had decided to burn them; first, however, he wanted me to bless them.

"This is my past," he said, "and I wish to forget it. Now I begin my life anew."

At nineteen or twenty, this is easier said than done. Not that Khi Young did not try—God knows, he tried hard enough. But there was still something twisted inside: and little by little, during the months that followed, this fact became painfully apparent to me.

Khi Young and I had breakfast together each morning. After assisting at Mass, Khi Young would hurry to the rectory and by the time I came over he would have a breakfast of toast, soft-boiled eggs, and coffee ready on the table. At the breakfast table he spoke frequently of the past. Some days he would go on at great length, but rarely would I interrupt him or prevent him. He said he had never mentioned these things to anyone before, and I felt that letting him pour out freely in words pent-up memories might act as a type of catharsis which in turn would ease some of the inner violence and fear still very much in evidence.

One morning he began speaking of his father; and by the time he finished his eyes were brimming over with tears. "*Sinbunim*," he said, "if I loved my father more, he would not have killed himself." Khi Young is still troubled by guilt feelings concerning the death of his father, and nothing I say seems to be able to dispel them.

"Father was a shipbuilder," he began, "a good one. When the Japanese were in Pusan he had a good job and our family lived well. The Japanese left in 1945, and this was followed by an immediate slump in the shipbuilding industry. Father's position and income declined steadily. Stepmother was a real *kaesaekki* [son of a bitch; one of Khi Young's favorite expressions]. Every evening she would yell and scream at Father for bringing home so little money. Father began to drink and this was his downfall. Little by little it got the better of him until finally he was no longer able to work. He would sit all day in a corner of the room trembling and staring into space. In the morning, if he did not first drink a cup of wine he could not eat his rice; but my stepmother refused to give him even a thimbleful to drink. He would beg and plead; and my sister, my brother, and I would beg and plead; but my stepmother's heart was stone. *Chaebal puthak haessumnida*—we pleaded and pleaded; but she always refused.

"One day I was alone in the house with Father. He ordered me to bring in the big knife from the kitchen and made me sit on the floor in front of him. Looking straight into my eyes, he took the knife and plunged it into the wooden floor just missing my leg. I can still remember the sound of the knife striking the floor, and I can still see it quivering back and forth. I was scared but would not let Father know it. I looked back into his face without blinking and without changing expression."

How old was Khi Young at this time? Eleven, he said.

He continued: "One afternoon I was playing with friends in an alley when suddenly a boy ran up to me and blurted out the news that my father had just drowned in Pusan Bay. The news made little impression on me. At first I thought that my father was drunk and had merely fallen into the water. I continued playing, but after a while I decided I might as well take a look. I walked over to the pier where Father lay. A large group of people had gathered about him but when they saw me coming they stepped aside to let me in. I looked at Father: his body was swollen and purple and I knew he was dead. But still it made no impression on me; I looked at the scene as would a third person, dry-eyed and with no feeling.

"I remember clearly how my stepmother was beating the ground with her fist, pulling out her hair, crying, and protesting to all onlookers what a good wife and good mother she was, and how could her husband be so ungrateful as to do such a thing? My only thought at the time was: Stepmother is a very good actress and an even better liar.

"Father's body was brought home, and the next day I, as eldest son, accompanied it to the crematorium near Somyon. I watched with no emotion as the body was burned over an electric fire. Then I gathered up the bones and smashed them into little pieces with a hammer. I took these, together with the ashes, to the top of a mountain near Somyon and sprinkled them to the four winds."

Here Khi Young paused and grew thoughtful. Then he looked up at me with a half-smile on his face and asked: "*Sinbunim*, will you do the same thing for me when I die? Will you see to it that my body is burned and the bones and ashes sprinkled on the mountaintop?" I smiled at this request and made no attempt to reply. Khi Young continued: "After coming down from the mountain I went home and lay down to rest. Then without warning tears burst from my eyes and for two days I cried uncontrollably. Then I stopped and it was all over."

At this point Khi Young produced from his shirt a cracked, fading photograph and held it out for me to look at. It was a photograph of his family and showed his father, sister, brother, and himself—all standing in solemn poses. His stepmother, too, figured in the photograph; but she was unrecognizable,

for her face had been scratched out with the point of a dirty
fountain pen. I asked Khi Young about it. Once again his face
took on that broken, enigmatic smile which I have come to
know so well, and he explained: "If I look at her face, I feel
bad."

On two occasions after his father's death, Khi Young himself attempted suicide by taking huge doses of sleeping pills;
but both times his stomach betrayed him and the pills came up.
He explained to me that he was constantly tormented by
various phobias, obsessions, and nightmares, and he had no
one and nothing to turn to for solace except death.

"A child," he said, "who experiences fear and pain will run
to his mother. The mother will embrace the child and in his
mother's arms a child's fear and pain dissolve. Since I have no
true mother to go to for comfort, I run to the thought of death.
For me, only in death's embrace will fear and pain dissolve
and disappear."

Khi Young's life with his stepmother, as has already been
touched on, was a little on the traumatic side. One day, for
example, Khi Young was caught by his stepmother taking food
from the kitchen. After beating him, she tied him to the wall
and kept him tied up for nearly a week.

One fine day in spring Khi Young, who was then fifteen,
became restless and ran away from home. He hopped a freight
train and eventually made his way to Seoul. The life of boy-
wanderer proved to be somewhat less romantic than he had
pictured it. After arriving in Seoul he slept in alleys and for
four days went without eating.

"Do you know," Khi Young said, "sometimes you can become so hungry you no longer feel hungry. Your mind becomes light and marvelously clear. This is the way it was in
Seoul."

After a while in Seoul, Khi Young made friends with another boy of eight or nine who was living off the streets like
himself. Khi Young shared with him the scraps of food which
he had collected from garbage cans, and at night they slept

together in the same place. This sense of charity toward those poorer than himself was one of the saving graces in Khi Young's life; and during the months he was with me I saw many touching manifestations of it.

After a few months of sleeping in alleys and eating out of garbage cans, life with stepmother did not look quite as unattractive as before, and Khi Young returned to Pusan. After a while he found work in a small iron foundry at Yongdo.

In Korea child labor is often exploited. So it was with Khi Young. He received a paltry salary of five dollars for working ten hours a day, seven days a week.

Since he did not have enough money to buy lunch, Khi Young habitually went without eating at noon. He had to swing a heavy long-stem hammer onto a metal rivet held in position by another older workman, and by two or three in the afternoon he was usually completely exhausted. One afternoon, dizzy from exhaustion, Khi Young kept missing the rivet. The older workman warned him; but Khi Young has a stubborn streak and the more he was warned the more he would miss the rivet. Finally the workman, baited beyond endurance, sprang to his feet and planted a foot against Khi Young's chest which sent him flying backward into a heavy metal machine.

Khi Young went black with shock and pain. Upon recovering, he picked himself up, grabbed the hammer, and went for the workman. "I would have killed him," he said, "if they had not pulled me off him in time." This type of incident, with colorful variations, was the story of his life. It is hardly surprising that the longest he ever held a job was eight months.

One day someone unjustly accused Khi Young of stealing a blanket. Khi Young, seething with anger, sought to balance the scales of justice with instant retribution. He got hold of a can of machine dye and emptied its contents in his accuser's water supply. Fortunately for Khi Young, his sister had seen him doing it and she poured out the water before any damage was done.

Everything in his life, however, was not grim; there were lighter moments. For example, there was the time he went on a moonlight picnic with the teenage gang which he palled around with.

"One night in summer," he began, "the gang stole some rice and we decided to climb to the top of Yongdo Mountain to cook it. The moon had not come up yet and the night was pitch-dark. You could not see your hand in front of your face. After getting to the top of the mountain we felt around with our hands, pulling up dried grass to use as fuel. But then we realized we had brought nothing to cook the rice in. Nevertheless, we kept feeling around on the ground and finally someone came across a shallow circular container—we were in luck. With this we scraped up water from the bed of a nearly dried-up stream; and, after washing the rice, we left it in the container and made preparations to cook it. Then the moon came up and we saw what the container was: it was the base of a human skull. After cooking and eating the rice, we took turns putting the skull on our heads and kicking it around just to prove that we were not afraid."

As was mentioned before, when the family split up, Khi Young's younger brother went to live with distant relatives who wanted the boy for work in their toy factory. On several occasions he came to the rectory to visit Khi Young. The boy was fifteen years old, but his constitution looked very weak and undeveloped. Khi Young explained to me that from the time he was two or three years old he had been suffering from a chronic ear illness, and this no doubt accounted for his pale, sickly appearance. I sent the boy to the hospital for an examination to see if anything could be done for him. Word came back that he was suffering from a serious ear infection and unless he was operated on very soon his life would be in danger. I agreed to pay expenses and the operation was subsequently performed. Khi Young's younger brother, although in much pain, thoroughly enjoyed his stay in the hospital; clean bed, good food, nice service—he had never had it so good, and, when I came to visit him once, he expressed the hope that his period of convalescence would be a long one.

Khi Young was touchingly devoted to his younger brother and he did his best to take care of him. After he left the hospital, the relatives whom he had been staying with previously refused to take him back, so I arranged for him to stay in a rented room very near the rectory. After recovering from the ear operation, he went back to work in the toy factory.

Shortly after his arrival in the parish, Khi Young began attending catechism class and studying Christian doctrine. During the day, moreover, I would often see him reading the Bible or saying the rosary in church. He was trying hard to make something of himself, but it was quite a struggle.

One day a boy in the parish had the misfortune to pick a fight with Khi Young. Although bigger and heavier than Khi Young, the boy left the field of battle with a blackened eye and a badly smashed face. Khi Young himself, except for some bruised knuckles, was virtually unscathed. One night a week or so later, the boy with the black eye waylaid Khi Young and, without warning, sent a fist smashing into his eye. The next morning Khi Young looked terrible: one eye was closed and the side of his face badly discolored. I would see him in the kitchen carefully studying his bruised countenance in the mirror. The more he looked at himself, he said, the angrier he got. Maybe it would be a good idea to summon the old gang from Yongdo; they would show the softies in this area a thing or two. For a while, we had the makings of a real rumble in the parish.

I called Khi Young into my room and, pointing to the floor, ordered him to kneel down. At first he just looked at me in surprise and stood there motionless. I repeated the order, and this time he knelt down.

"Now promise me," I said, "as long as you are in this parish you won't get into any more fights?" He hesitated and then in a small voice he said: "*Sinbunim*, as long as I am staying with you I promise not to do any more fighting." Although afterward there were moments of almost superhuman temptation, Khi Young—except for one or two minor slips—stuck by his promise.

Khi Young often mentioned to me his desire to study and so I gave him his chance. I arranged for a college graduate, who was then employed in my fund-raising office downtown, to tutor him, but it didn't work out. Khi Young had long lost the habit of regular disciplined study, and he couldn't stick to it.

For that matter, he couldn't stick to much of anything. He would begin something, get as far as the middle, then give up. I realized he was sick inside, but didn't quite know what to do about it.

After a while I made arrangements for Khi Young to work in my office downtown, running errands, filing cards, cleaning up, and doing other odd jobs. Against the advice of everyone, I entrusted him with large sums of money. My confidence in him flattered him and I thought it would help him psychologically. I was well aware of his dead-end kid background and I realized the risk that I was running. Under the circumstances, however, I thought it the best thing to do. As it turned out, it may have been a mistake.

At any rate, one Monday afternoon about $200 worth of stamps mysteriously disappeared from our office. All the circumstantial evidence pointed to one person and one person only. That was Khi Young, of course. I called him in and questioned him. In tears he said that he knew nothing about it. I took him at his word and let it go at that.

From this point on, he went from bad to worse. One day, for example, I came home from retreat to find the house a complete shambles. Khi Young met me at the door and abjectly begged for forgiveness. He explained that in a fit of depression he drank of bottle of *soju* (local rotgut) and, thus fortified, decided to wreck everything.

More and more in his conversation one phrase would recur: *"Sarami nomu manhsumnida"* (too many people). Also the subject of suicide and death cropped up more frequently. Khi Young said he would like to eat TNT and blow up not only himself but all those around him as well. He was fascinated by fire and explosives and, without my knowing it, he tried on several occasions to get a job as dynamiter in an iron mine near Pusan. He also offered his services to some river fishermen who were illegally using dynamite to blow up fish. Happily he did not succeed in these attempts.

I tried to plant some hope in Khi Young's heart, but it was not easy. "If I get a good job," he would say, "then what?" "Well," I would answer, "then you get married and raise a fine family."

"Then what?"

"Well, then you can have a normal happy life."

"Then what?"

At which point I would give up. Khi Young was pathologically afraid of bringing into the world a family such as his father had done. Like father like son, he thought; and the tragedy which had happened in the case of the father could just as easily happen in the case of the son.

I was convinced that Khi Young was in need of professional treatment. After some inquiry I was given the address of a good psychiatrist in Pusan, who had studied at the University of Wisconsin in the States. Psychiatric treatment, even in Korea, is expensive and there is no guarantee of its outcome. Still, there seemed to be no alternative; so I decided to give it a try.

Before making an appointment, however, I asked Khi Young, who had been with me a year and a half now, if he would follow my instructions. Yes, he said, he would do anything I told him to. Then I informed him of my decision to take him to a psychiatrist. He swallowed hard at this, but after a little persuasion he agreed to go.

After arriving at the psychiatrist's office I spent thirty minutes alone with him telling him about Khi Young and answering the doctor's questions. Then I went out and left Khi

Young with him for approximately the same length of time. Khi Young came out and I went in again, this time to learn the diagnosis.

The psychiatrist spoke in English. "This boy is very sick," he said, "what's more, he's dangerous. If he were in the United States, by law he would have to be committed to an institution." Khi Young may be dangerous, I said, but to himself —not to others. The doctor corrected me. "The tendency to suicide and homicide," he explained, "is one and the same— only the direction is different. In Khi Young's case, this tendency, although now apparently self-directed, can suddenly and without warning become other-directed."

When did the doctor think that Khi Young should be committed? Immediately, he said. How long would he have to remain in the hospital? It was hard to say; maybe six months, maybe eight months. What if he refused? In that case, he should be committed by force.

I went out to the waiting room and sat down on the bench beside Khi Young. I looked at him and asked the question I had asked before taking him to see the psychiatrist: "*Nae sikhinundaero hagessumnikka?*" Will you do whatever I tell you? He answered with a feeble, "Yes." Then I told him he would have to stay in the hospital for a while. Before the news had a chance to register, I took him by the arm and led him into the doctor's office. From there we passed through another door into the interior of a small mental hospital which the doctor maintained. As we entered, the inmates, about fifteen or twenty in number and all in various states of dementia, gathered around to inspect the new arrival. Before Khi Young had time even to think, he was on the inside of a mental institute looking out. It was a dizzying experience. Finally, Khi Young gathered his wits about him and started to protest.

"*Sinbunim,*" he said, "*usopji anhsumnikka?*" (Isn't this laughable?) There was a look of stark terror in his eyes—a look which I found hard to meet. I tried to reason with him. Finally, Khi Young took another tack and asked if he could not go home for a few days, arrange his affairs, and return quietly on Monday. He promised solemnly that if I were to let him out, he *would* come back on Monday.

Then with some misgivings and against the doctor's advice I took Khi Young back to Songdo with me. Upon leaving, the doctor looked at him with a worried, non-professional look and told him not to get into any fights. Khi Young asked me later what he had meant by this. I was hard put for an explanation.

Before leaving, I had an interesting talk with the doctor concerning mental breakdowns in Korea. I was always of the opinion that mental illness was much more widespread among the tension-prone, fast-living, high-stepping citizens of the U.S. than in Korea, where the pace is considerably slower. The doctor assured me that this was nonsense. One of the principal causes of mental breakdown, he pointed out, is the absence of hope for the future. Most Americans, no matter how difficult the present, can usually find something to hope for in the future. Such is not the case with Koreans. Because the country is so poverty-stricken, the future looks black, without opportunity, and, in a sense, hopeless. This absence of hope, more than anything else, is responsible for many breakdowns in Korea. The fact that in Korea there are few psychiatrists, and still fewer facilities for treating the mentally ill does not call attention to the problem; nevertheless, concluded the doctor, the incidence of psychic illness in Korea is considerably higher than in the States.

The Sunday before Khi Young was to go back to the hospital was a memorable one. In the evening, he stole the keys to my jeep and both Khi Young and jeep disappeared. He took a friend along for the joy ride. They bought a bottle of wine and, between them, emptied its contents. A little after midnight, Khi Young, jeep, and friend—all a little hung over —made it safely back to the church.

The next morning after Mass I came over for breakfast. To my surprise, breakfast was ready as usual, but there was no

Khi Young. Instead there was a message scrawled across the kitchen blackboard which read: "Gone swimming. Will be back shortly. Khi Young." It was already the middle of September and the swimming season had ended several weeks before. Worried, I thought of going to look for him, but I had no idea where to begin. So I entrusted the matter to his angel and sat down to breakfast.

An hour or so later Khi Young returned. He was blue in the face and his teeth were chattering—but he was smiling happily. He said he had had an enjoyable swim. I said I was glad of that; now get ready because in an hour we're leaving for the hospital.

An hour later I entered his room, and, of course, nothing was ready. It was his considered opinion, moreover, that instead of going to the hospital today it would be much better if he went tomorrow or the next day.

I picked up a small bag, threw underwear, socks, toothbrush, and some books into it, and said: "Let's go." I took him to the hospital, signed the necessary papers, and had him committed. As I was to find out later, however, putting a patient in a hospital is one thing, making him stay is another.

A few days later I myself had to leave for the U.S. on some urgent diocesan business for Bishop Choi. I was away a month. While in the States I received a written report from the psychiatrist in Pusan in which he informed me that he had been giving Khi Young electric shock treatments and tranquilizers. According to the doctor, little by little Khi Young seemed to be emerging from his inner psychotic world into the real world outside. This sounded encouraging.

Upon returning to Pusan, however, I learned that Khi Young had escaped from the hospital the week before and was then staying with friends at Yongdo. He had been phoning the rectory every morning to find out if I had returned yet.

A few days later while I was in the kitchen preparing supper Khi Young showed up. I was shocked by the way he looked, but tried hard not to show it. He had a slightly demented,

Mongoloid aspect. His hair was wildly disheveled, the pupils of his eyes exaggeratedly dilated, and the flesh on his face oddly puffed up and swollen. When he began to talk, his speech seemed thick, and the words came out slowly and painfully. I learned later that these symptoms were the result of the electric shock, the tranquilizers, and, most of all, heavy doses of sleeping tablets which Khi Young had been taking on his own.

I asked Khi Young the reason why he had run away from the hospital. Because of the electric shock, however, his memory was partially gone and, try as he would, he could not think of it. I told him he could stay with me for one week. At the end of that time, if he refused to return to the hospital, he would have to leave.

The next afternoon I got in my jeep and drove across town to visit the psychiatrist who had been treating Khi Young. The psychiatrist was very apologetic concerning Khi Young's escape and embarrassed for letting it happen. He then suggested that I bring the patient back by force. This I refused to do. Either he came back on his own—or not at all. The doctor shrugged his shoulders and then warned me strongly to keep out of Khi Young's sight anything which might be used as a lethal instrument. I thought of the big ten-inch bread knife in the kitchen and resolved to hide it. As I was leaving, the doctor gave me some personal effects which Khi Young had deposited with him upon his entry into the hospital.

After returning home I went through these effects and came across a very interesting item. It was a postal savings passbook. On July 1, about the same time the $200 worth of stamps had disappeared from the office, Khi Young's passbook showed that a deposit in the same amount had been made in his postal savings account.

That evening I called him into my room and without comment handed him the passbook. He opened it slowly, and his eyes fell on the July 1 entry; and, at the same time, in a corner of his mind a memory stirred. He looked at me, and I looked back at him; and for the first time he knew that I knew.

He began to cry. Then, putting the passbook in his mouth, he savagely tore it apart with his teeth and, lifting up the lid of the stove, flung it into the fire.

Why had he done it? Khi Young could not remember. What had he used the money for? He was not sure of that either; but he thought he had used most of it on his brother. He had bought him a radio, new clothes, new shoes. He asked me to forgive him.

"If," he said, "a person with no hands and arms is given chopsticks and a bowl of rice, no matter how hard that person tries he cannot eat the rice. It is the same with me, *Sinbunim*; no matter how hard I try to be good, I cannot succeed. I lack the hands and arms. In other words, I lack the habit."

Khi Young desperately wanted me to punish him: beat him, kick him, scold him—do something. But, as for any punishment, Khi Young himself was his worst chastiser. And, besides, who can judge where mental sickness ends and moral responsibility begins? Khi Young, I felt, was more to be pitied than blamed; all the more so, since he himself was completely incapable of self-pity. At any rate, he said now that I finally knew the truth he felt better. "*Maumi siwon hamnida.*" (My heart is cool.)

When Khi Young's week was up, he refused to return to the hospital. He had an almost animal terror of electric shock treatment and nothing I said could persuade him to go back. He left the rectory then and went to live with his brother.

I heard nothing from Khi Young for several weeks; then one evening I received a phone call from him. "*Sinbunim,*" he said, "*mian hamnida! mian hamnida! mian hamnida!*" (I'm sorry!) Then he lost control and cried. For the next few minutes, all that came over the receiver was the sound of a painful, choked, dry sobbing. I told him to come and see me, and a half hour later he showed up at the rectory.

He looked terrible, much worse than the first time I saw him after his escape from the hospital. Khi Young told me that he had decided to kill himself on Saturday. It was then Thursday. During the last few weeks he had been spending his days going from one pharmacy to another collecting enough Sekinol tablets to put himself asleep permanently. He had attempted suicide three times before and failed—this time he wanted to succeed. I asked Khi Young to bring me the medicine which he had been collecting. At first he refused. After considerable persuasion, however, he left the rectory and returned a little later with the medicine. It was wrapped in a piece of old newspaper. I opened the package and counted twenty-five bright red Sekinol tablets, more than enough to kill an ordinary person. Khi Young asked me please not to throw the medicine away because it was expensive and, besides, it was not easy to get. I put the medicine in my desk drawer and locked it.

Then I turned to Khi Young and tried to persuade him to return to the hospital. I was sure that if Khi Young continued the way he was going he would end up doing violence to himself—or to others. Finally his resistance broke down and he said that, okay, if it would make me happy he would go back.

A few days later I drove him back to the hospital. When he saw the place again he balked, and a look of terror came over his face. Actually, there was a misunderstanding: there was another mental hospital in Pusan, and, for some reason or another, Khi Young thought that I was taking him there, not to the place where he formerly was. I shrugged my shoulders and—against my better judgment—drove him to the other hospital and had him admitted. This hospital turned out to be an "ongthori pyongwon" (a quack hospital). But I didn't find this out until a couple of months later.

Khi Young was content with his new surroundings. He was free to come and go as he pleased; and, above all, there was no electric shock machine.

One day, however, he turned up at the rectory in a state of near-hysteria. His closest friend—whom I myself had met on a couple of occasions—had taken poison and killed himself. Khi Young had just been informed of the fact; and, before even going to pay his respects to the body, he had come to see me. He wanted an answer to one question: "Is my friend in hell now?" I told him that this was a question which only God could answer.

Khi Young went to see his friend and later he described his visit to me in detail. He had placed his hand on the forehead of his dead friend and held it there for a long time. It felt cool, like marble, he said. The death of his friend was a deep emotional shock, and after this Khi Young's usual nightmares and crying spells increased sharply.

After a while at the hospital they decided it might be better to keep Khi Young locked up, but they didn't know him very well. After a few days of confinement, he broke out. By this time, for a number of reasons, I had lost all confidence in this hospital. So I decided to take Khi Young back to live with me—at least temporarily.

He seemed a little better now, but not much. He was melancholy, impulsive, and still very much obsessed by the idea of suicide. "*Sinbunim,*" he explained, "if someone has a knife in his belly, even though he realizes that it will be worse if he pulls it out, he cannot help himself—he must pull it out." Khi Young reasoned that even after suicide if it would get worse and he would go to hell, his inner life had become so unbearable that he could no longer help himself.

I wanted him to go back to the first hospital where he had been treated, but he was still terrified by the thought of electric shock and refused. After a few days, suspecting something, I asked Khi Young if he had any money left. No, he said, he was broke. How about sleeping pills, then, or other drugs? No, he had nothing. I didn't take his word for it. Later in the day, when Khi Young was out (I learned afterward that he was in the church library reading a book on purgatory), I searched his room but found nothing.

The next morning after Mass when I came over for breakfast

I found Khi Young lying on his bed unconscious. His breathing was heavy and labored, and there was a trickle of white foam on his lips. On his desk I found a suicide note addressed to me. Among other things the note contained the information that he had taken thirty-four Sekinol tablets. Later I learned that he had carefully hidden the medicine behind his desk.

I anointed him and sent him to the Pusan University Hospital. This was the second time around. Once again they put a stomach pump in him and began injecting serum into his bloodstream to flush out any toxic matter. Also they inserted a tube into his bladder to drain off excess fluid.

Fourteen hours after he was admitted Khi Young began coming out of the coma. He kept repeating over and over the number "*solhun-naegae*" (thirty-four).

Shortly after Khi Young regained consciousness, I went to see him. He was a sight. After he had taken the Sekinol, apparently he had fallen against the metal stove in his room because one side of his face was burned and badly swollen and his arm and shoulder on the same side had been injured. His eyes can best be described as two dark wounds of pain.

He looked at me, tried to smile, and then said he was sorry. In a pitiful voice he cried: "*Sinbunim*, why can I not die? I took thirty-four tablets and still I am not dead."

It was a good question. For a normal person half that number would have been enough to do the job. The only explanation is that over the years Khi Young had taken so many drugs and sleeping pills that his organism had built up a strong resistance. Khi Young then told me that his friend, Choi Jin Il, who had committed suicide a month before, would be disappointed because he had planned to be with him by now.

After a while a doctor came to examine Khi Young's arm and shoulder to see if any bones had been broken. The doctor's bedside manner was none too gentle and Khi Young cursed him softly under his breath. The doctor announced that nothing was broken and said that Khi Young could leave.

In passing, I would like to cite the warm spirit of charity which reigns at the Pusan University Hospital. You pull up to the emergency entrance with a dying patient and the first thing they ask you for is a deposit of money to cover future medical expenses. You have to pay cash on the barrel-head before they will even look at the patient. And if you don't have it? Well, patients have been known to die waiting for treatment outside of the emergency ward, while relatives tried in vain to raise enough money for admission deposit.

In the same room with Khi Young were two other suicide-attempt cases. One was a girl in her early twenties. Although a little short of money when she arrived, she was admitted anyhow. She recovered quickly, and when she was discharged the next day the hospital authorities confiscated her overcoat to make up the shortage. Weak, shivering, and penniless, the young lady walked out of the hospital into the cold February morning air.

But to get back to Khi Young, although still very weak and unsteady, he walked out of the hospital on his own steam. I helped him into the jeep and drove away. He thought I was taking him back to the parish, but he was mistaken. Instead I drove him to the mental hospital where he was first treated and had made some progress. He protested, but was really too weak to offer much resistance. So I had him admitted without too much trouble. But Khi Young still had plenty of fight left in him and as I was leaving the hospital he announced that, effective immediately, he was going on a hunger strike. He lasted about a week, and then little by little he began eating again.

Life is full of surprises, and among the more pleasant ones of late is the remarkable progress Khi Young has been making since he re-entered the hospital. He is responding very well to the electric shock treatment and other therapy which he has been receiving. Little by little he seems to be coming out of his depression, apathy, and psychosis into the warmth and light of the real everyday world. His will to live is growing stronger, and now he even possesses a certain *joie de vivre*, something I could never find in him before. Most important of all, the seed of hope has taken root in his heart and he is making plans for the future. He wants to learn English and typing, so he can get a job in my office. Later on, he plans to get married and raise a family.

As if to show his gratitude to me, Khi Young has been a real apostle of late among the other inmates of the mental hospital. Thanks to his efforts, three of these have promised to take instruction after they are discharged; and, another young man, a former fallen-away Catholic, has returned to the sacraments.

I try to visit Khi Young once every week or ten days. Every time I see him I must extract from him anew the promise that he will not try to break out. Three months have gone by now, and during this time not once has he attempted to escape. This in itself borders on the miraculous.

The doctor tells me that in another three or four months Khi Young should be ready for discharge. This is good news indeed.

Until now, Khi Young certainly has given his Guardian Angel an incredibly devilish time of it. The Angel, however, has taken uncommonly good care of this badly mixed-up, inwardly tormented, much-to-be-pitied young boy. Khi Young still has a rough road to travel before achieving full recovery. This time, however, with the continuing help of his angel and the grace of God, it looks like he will go all the way.

CHAPTER THIRTEEN

EVERYONE AGREES that the best way to help hungry people is to give them jobs so that they may help themselves. In Korea today, hungry people are many; jobs are few. As a matter of fact, forty per cent of the working population is either unemployed or underemployed.

As a partial answer to this problem, two years ago we began in Pusan a cottage-industry embroidery program. Now "Operation Hanky," as it is called, is a going concern. At present 2000 women in the Pusan area are at work on the project. Most of these are mothers of families. Some are widows. Some are paralytics. All are from the ranks of the poverty-stricken, the hungry, the needy.

How does "Operation Hanky" work? Basically, it combines two things: 1) American direct mail fund-raising techniques; and 2) the highly developed embroidery skill of the Korean women.

The women embroider an attractive Oriental design on Korean cotton cloth, which in turn is made into a lady's handkerchief. The finished product, along with an appeal letter, a folder, and of course the inevitable return envelope, is mailed to people in the United States. Donations are sent directly to Korea or to an intermediary office in the United States. Dollars thus earned by "Operation Hanky" are either put back into the program or they are used to support one of the many charities sponsored by Bishop Choi. This is the idea in capsule form; its practical implementation is somewhat more involved.

We began by selecting leaders in each of the twenty parishes in the general Pusan area. A leader is chosen according to her embroidery skill, sense of responsibility, and ability to handle people. After selection and training, the parish leader gives a sewing test to the poor women in her area desirous of working on the program. Whether these women are Catholic or non-Catholic is irrelevant; the important thing is that they be poor and capable of doing the work. Needless to say, there is always a wide gap between the number of women desirous of work and the amount of work actually available—but we are doing our best to remedy this situation.

After passing the initial sewing test, the women are given a place on the program. At the beginning of each day the parish leader distributes cloth material to the sewers in her area. The sewers take this material home and fit the embroidery work into their normal daily household routine. The fact that the women can do the work at home while at the same time watching the children and preparing the family meals is one of its more attractive features.

The embroidered cloth is then brought back to the leader, who in turn takes it to a central office for inspection and payment. At our central office it is cut, trimmed, edged, and transformed into a lady's handkerchief. The finished product is then packaged and made ready for shipment to people in the United States. Korean women are skillful with needle and thread, and the finished handkerchief is an attractive and desirable item. The reaction of those receiving it in the United States has been quite favorable.

Sewers employed by "Operation Hanky" earn as much as 5000 won a month. This is most generous, especially when one considers that factory-employed women in Korea rarely earn more than 3000 won a month and also when one considers that "Operation Hanky" was conceived only as a means of providing a side income.

This program is very popular with the women working on it. For example, recently one of our staff visited a young paralytic woman near Pusan who was working at home on "Operation Hanky." In this case "home" was a lean-to constructed of mud, scrap wood, and tar paper. When asked about the program, the woman, hugging the embroidery frame close to her, exclaimed with much emotion: "This is the first real work I have had in my life. You cannot imagine what it means to me. Pray God that it continues!"

We have every intention not only of continuing but also expanding the program. This year we will mail out close to a million handkerchiefs. Next year we hope to double this number.

As was mentioned previously, "Operation Hanky" uses direct mail fund-raising techniques which—especially since the end of the Second World War—have been highly developed in the United States. Some people frown on this method of getting money. If they themselves receive an appeal containing "unsolicited merchandise" they contemptuously refer to it as "junk mail," and a cry goes up to heaven that their name has found its way onto another "sucker list."

I confess that at one time I, too, was squeamish about this method of raising funds. I thought it was like putting a knife to people's throats, whereas Christian charity should be free and spontaneous. This was before I came to Korea and was named pastor of a destitute and hungry flock. In such an environment it is surprising how quickly one loses his scruples. I now find myself saying: So what's wrong with putting a knife to people's throats? They've got it, your own people need it and have a right to it, and there is no other way of getting it —so what's wrong with it? The fact that at least in our particular circumstances there *is* no other way of getting it should be emphasized.

Two years ago we ran a simple fund-raising test from Pusan. We mailed in equal quantities two items: 1) a straight appeal letter; and 2) the same letter plus the relatively inexpensive handsewn handkerchief. The returns were very enlightening. Only seven per cent of those receiving the straight letter sent in donations, as opposed to a whopping thirty-three per cent of those who received the letter plus the handkerchief. In other words, more than four times as many people were willing to donate when they received a "premium" enclosed in their appeal letter than when they did not. The subtle pyschological pressure of an inexpensive gift enclosed in a fund-raising package is not to be gainsaid or denied. Charity—free, cheerful, and spontaneous—is a lovely concept. Unfortunately, lovely concepts do not fill hungry bellies. It has been my experience that you have to lean on people just a little in order to induce them to perform what is really an obligation in justice; namely, giving out of their superabundance to the poor and hungry of the world.

While "Operation Hanky" copies freely mail fund-raising methods used in the United States, still in many respects it differs. For one thing our profit-cost breakdown is considerably better than that of most Stateside fund-raisers.

"Operation Hanky" operates on a ninety-eight to two per cent profit-cost ratio. In other words, ninety-eight per cent of the donated dollar goes directly for the purpose for which it is given, namely to help the Korean economy. A marginal two per cent goes for miscellaneous operating expenses incurred in the United States.

Another slightly different aspect of "Operation Hanky" is its old-fashioned, amateurish approach. For one thing, everything is done by hand labor. In our office in Pusan there are no 707 and 1501 computers or other fancy electronic gear—just people. During my business trip to the United States I had occasion to visit the headquarters of a highly successful priest fund-raiser. He was installed in an impressive three-story building equipped with the latest electronic gadgetry. The priest showed me about the premises and we came to one monster 1984-type machine which he had just purchased to address his mail and to handle his list of donors. I asked the price of the machine and was told it cost $500,000. I whistled and then said: "Father, in Korea we do everything by hand. We address by hand; assemble by hand; put the stamp on the envelope by hand; file and post by hand. Nonetheless, I am willing to bet that this method is not only far cheaper but also more efficient than the $500,000 electronic machine." Since I myself have had experience with electronic computers, I could make such a claim without fear of being contradicted. What is more, the average donor in the United States is more receptive to a personal hand-addressed letter than to one which is the product of an electronic machine. This homey, personal touch to "Operation Hanky" is another factor contributing to its success.

Where does the money received from "Operation Hanky" go? As has already been pointed out, "Operation Hanky" is its own justification. Much of the money, therefore, goes right back into the program, creating more work for needy people and putting more money into circulation in the Korean economy.

But in addition to maintaining and expanding the embroidery program itself, there has been a healthy surplus of funds which have gone into other relief projects. With the money received from "Operation Hanky," to date we have built one hospital, two dispensaries, an orphanage, an old-age home, and a boys' technical school. We have also launched an irrigation project and a cooperative farm program. In addition to this, we have given direct grants of money to over thirty hospitals, leper colonies, orphanages, schools, and other works of charity scattered throughout Korea.

In conjunction with funds raised through "Operation Hanky," one phase of relief work we wish to concentrate on in particular is orphan welfare. Of all the poor, helpless, and destitute people in Korea, the poorest, the most helpless, and the most destitute is the orphan child. Not only does the orphan child lack the physical and material necessities of life, but what is more, he lacks also the spiritual and psychological requisites of a full life; namely, a mother's love and the warmth of a family.

Orphan work is a biblical charity, in the sense that we find frequent mention of it in the pages of both the Old and the New Testament. For example, in the Book of Psalms, God refers to Himself in a most touching way as "the Father of orphans." It is, perhaps, because the orphan child is so utterly helpless and defenseless that God favors him with special love and attention.

In Korea, at present, the orphan situation is bad, and getting worse. It is estimated that there are 70,000 children living in orphanages scattered throughout the country. In addition to this number, many more parentless, homeless youngsters are living on and off the streets of Korea's big cities. The practice of child abandonment, moreover, is also rapidly increasing. In 1964, 8000 children were abandoned in Korea; and all indications are that in 1965 this figure will be still higher. It is not that Korean parents do not love their children, but the sound of a child's voice in the house crying for food when there is no food can make even the most devoted parent do strange things. Also many poverty-stricken parents reason—rightly or wrongly —that their child will have a better chance in an orphanage than if he remains with them at home.

I myself have visited many orphanages in Korea. Some are excellent institutions. Others are pretty pathetic.

In this latter category, I remember in particular an orphanage I visited recently in Masan. In each room I found children, ranging from three to twelve, sitting next to each other in closed ranks. A mattress had been placed on their hands and legs, and an older orphan girl was standing in front of them, menacingly holding a stick in her hand. The children normally should have been romping and playing. Instead they just sat there in stony silence staring vacantly into space with a look in their eyes compounded of emptiness, confusion, and fear. It was rather appalling to see.

I use this as an example of the pathetic type of orphanage. But even an excellent orphanage is still an orphanage and at best can offer a child only a cold, institutional, slightly inhuman type of existence. In such an environment it is difficult for a child to develop into a happy, healthy, smiling youngster. Most orphanage inmates seem to be emotionally starved creatures. More than food itself, they crave a mother's love and they crave it with a deep hunger of the soul which is quite painful to see.

In an American university some time ago experiments were conducted with baby monkeys, the results of which are more or less applicable to humans also. Three just-born monkeys were placed in a cage containing two mannequins. One mannequin was covered with fur and made to resemble in every way a real-live mother monkey. The other mannequin was made of wire; but, attached to the wire were baby bottles full of life-giving milk. The baby monkeys, without exception, turned away from the wire contraption with the milk and huddled for warmth and security against the fur of the mannequin resembling the mother monkey. If left alone, the monkeys in the experiment would have starved to death while clinging to the fur of the mother mannequin. The moral of the story is obvious: a mother's love is more vital to an infant than food itself.

This is one of the underlying principles of the family-unit orphanage program which we are just now beginning in Pusan.

The idea of the *Maria Pomohwe* (Maria Orphan-Mother Society), as it is called, arose from two current facts of life in Korea. On one hand there is a large number of Catholic girls who desire to enter the convent, but are prevented by either lack of middle and high school education or by lack of funds. On the other hand there is a crying need for dedicated personnel in the field of orphan welfare. So why not put the two together and begin a movement dedicated exclusively to the care of orphan children? In so doing, many dedicated young Catholic girls, who otherwise would be prevented, will be permitted to realize a religious vocation which they feel is theirs. And at the same time neglected orphan children will benefit immensely by receiving that special love and attention which only totally dedicated women can give.

I began by placing a notice in the Catholic Shibo, a Korea-wide Catholic weekly paper, and by sending out letters to all the parishes in Korea asking for volunteers. Applicants had to be between the ages of twenty-four and thirty-five, primary school graduates, and baptized for at least three years. Seventy-five girls applied; and eleven were selected to begin the program. Next year we will be able to accept twice this number.

A small training center, adjacent to the parish church, was prepared. A Korean Benedictine Sister was placed in charge of formation. By special permission, the Sister in charge of formation was allowed to take her meals with the future orphan-mothers and to live in the same quarters.

The training program is very simple and strives to combine the practical with the speculative. Mornings are devoted to study and spiritual formation. The future orphan-mothers attend classes in child care, child psychology, Christian doctrine, Scripture, and ascetic theology. Afternoons are given over to practical training and work with orphan children. For this phase of the program, the girls are sent out to near-by orphanages.

After successfully completing a full year of training, the girls will make four promises: poverty, chastity, obedience, and a final promise to dedicate their lives to the service of orphan children. The orphan-mother will renew these promises each year for a period of three years; at the end of this time she will be permitted to make them permanently.

After making first promises, an orphan-mother will be assigned a small house and will be entrusted with five or six orphan children. The orphans, both boys and girls, will range in age from infants to children of five or six. The orphan-mother will be expected to mold this group into a real family unit. Her vocation is to give a mother's love and attention to the emotionally starved children entrusted to her. In so doing, the warmth and joy of true family life will be generated, and the orphans will have a chance to develop into normal people rather than soul-scarred alumni of institutions.

In passing, it should be mentioned that the idea of the "Maria Pomohwe" borrows heavily from the S.O.S. orphan-village program as developed in Austria, and also from Auxilium, a type of Secular Institute whose headquarters is located in Lourdes. Mostly, however, the idea is in response to local needs and was born in local context.

The story of the arrival of the first orphan child in our midst belongs to the "man proposes, God disposes" vein of literature. Man—in this case, myself—did not propose to accept orphan children until the future orphan-mothers had fully completed their training program. God's Providence, however, disposed otherwise, and we had no choice but to acquiesce.

It was a Friday in April, and I received word that a man was dying and wanted the Last Sacraments. The man had been sick for some time, I was told; and there was no hurry. But if *Sinbunim* were not too busy, a visit would be appreciated.

Later that same morning, carrying the Blessed Sacrament and the holy oils, I left the church and, after a twenty-minute climb up the side of a mountain, I came to a small cloth factory. The factory, about the size of an American garage, was made of pressed mud and had a tar-paper roof. When I entered, the people working inside stopped and looked up in wonder.

I glanced around and, in a far corner of the room, spotted a man lying on the floor in a bundle of rags. Next to him sat a small boy of five or six who I learned later was his son. The man, Matthew by name, was in his middle-fifties and was suffering from paralysis and some kind of mental illness. Some time ago Matthew had sold his house in order to get money for food. Since he was now sick and had no other place to live, the factory owner kindly offered Matthew the shelter of his workshop. The dying man's presence underfoot in no way interfered with production. The workers simply stepped around him and didn't think twice about the matter.

The only one who did think about the dying man was his son, Paullo. Paullo took care of his father's needs as best he could. He gave him water to drink when he was thirsty and food, begged from neighbors, to eat when he was hungry.

I have seen many poor people in Korea, but rarely have I seen anyone living in such squalor as this dying man and his small child. After returning to the parish, then, I sent the catechist back to learn the facts and to see what could be done to lift this man and his child out of their degradation.

The catechist returned that evening with a strange tale. Matthew's first wife had died several years ago, and shortly thereafter he took a second one, this time a girl of seventeen. A year ago Matthew contracted paralysis and at the same time a type of mental sickness called, in Korean, "*euichojong*" (wife-doubting sickness). "*Euichojong*" is not too uncommon in Korea and occurs especially when the wife is much younger than the husband. The sickness is characterized by a morbid, obsessive doubt of the wife's fidelity. Matthew, rendered partially mad and off-balance by his illness, took to torturing his young wife and beating the children. On one occasion, he tried to set fire to his house. A few months ago, the wife and all the children, except Paullo, ran away.

The neighbors, however, insisted to the catechist that Matthew was not sick at all but only pretending. As a matter of fact, after Sinbunim had anointed him and left the factory, the neighbors with their own eyes had seen Matthew get up and walk away smiling to his own house which was near by and still very much intact. In other words, according to the neighbors, Matthew was merely putting on an act in order to trick Sinbunim into giving him money.

This tale sounded unlikely and farfetched. But in Korea one hears many things which are unlikely and farfetched, and yet true. So, after listening to the catechist's report I shrugged my shoulders and decided to wait before taking further action.

I didn't have to wait long. Less than a week later, word came down from the mountain again, this time that the man had died. I sent the catechist back to investigate and this time he came back with a report far different from the one he had given previously. We had been deceived all right, not by Matthew, however, who really was dying, but by his neighbors.

Because of Matthew's mental sickness, he had done many things to injure his neighbors and some of these came to hate him with something akin to animal hatred. It was these who had invented the story that Matthew was faking, in order to prevent him from getting material help from the pastor. Apparently it afforded them pleasure to see this man die in filth and degradation like an animal.

It was a little late now, but the least we could do to make up for our unwitting mistake was to bury Matthew in dignity. And this we set out to do. Members of the parish Legion of Mary visited the factory and prepared the body for burial. They washed it, dressed it in clean clothes, and placed it in a wooden coffin which we had purchased. They then sat up all night beside the coffin praying and keeping vigil. The pagan neighbors were amazed by this simple, unassuming display of Christian love.

Paullo watched passively as his father's dead body was prepared for burial. He, too, remained beside the coffin all night —after all, he had no other place to go. A Legion member asked the small boy if he realized what had happened to his father. Yes, his father was dead, and he would see him no more. Now that his father was gone, how would Paullo live? He would go each day to a different neighbor and beg his rice; he would manage all right.

We scheduled Matthew's funeral for the morning after his death. We learned that Matthew had a thirteen-year-old daughter who was employed as housegirl by a well-to-do family in Pusan; but no one knew her exact whereabouts. We contacted the radio station and sent out a bulletin. And the young girl turned up in time for the funeral.

After the funeral we sent the young girl and her little brother off to Seoul in search of relatives with whom they might be able to live. Two days later they were back in Pusan. They had failed to locate the relatives and now had no place to go. As the girl sat in my office telling me of her trip and her futile search, tears streamed down her cheeks. Paullo sat next to his sister on a chair. His legs were crossed and folded under him and he had a grave expression on his face. There was something odd and strangely troubling about this youngster, but at first I could not put my finger on it. Then it came to me: he was not a child at all—he was a little man. Although his body was underdeveloped for a five-year-old, the expression on his face was that of a mature man. This youngster had seen so much of the other side of life in five short years that psychically he had passed from infant to adult without the happy transition of childhood.

What was I to do with this crying girl and the little boy with the man's expression? I could place the child in an orphanage and arrange for his sister to return to the family where she had been previously employed. But for a number of reasons I was reluctant to do this. So I had one of the Sisters in the parish prepare a small room for them near the church and I made arrangements for our future orphan-mothers to give them their meals and watch over them.

Later, the girl told me she had another brother, eleven years old, who was living on the streets of Pusan with a gang of shoe-shine boys. We set out to locate him. After a few days we learned that he had been picked up by police and placed in an orphanage on the outskirts of Pusan. We contacted the orphanage director and requested that the child be released and permitted to rejoin his older sister and younger brother. The orphanage director agreed—provided we pay him a certain sum of money.

This particular orphanage, like many others, received a subsidy from the government and other relief agencies based on the number of children in the institution. This subsidy was usually less than the bare minimum necessary to keep the children in good health. By maintaining, however, a submarginal standard of living in his orphanage, an unscrupulous director could exploit those under him and make a nice personal profit for himself. This is a sordid way of making a living, perhaps; but then many un-pretty things happen in the world of the poor. With regard to Paullo's brother, however, we refused to pay. Instead, we tried exerting a little pressure in the right places and Paullo's brother was subsequently released—free of charge.

That evening I paid a visit to our orphan family to see how the new arrival was making out. Jin Gap, as he is called, was clad only in shorts, and he got up quickly when I arrived. I was startled by what I saw. Spindly arms and legs, caved-in chest, protruding belly—he was a real case of malnutrition. He was also infected with skin disease. To make matters worse he had that orphan look in his eyes—a look compounded of terror, fear, and distrust.

On the occasion of that same visit, however, I had the immense pleasure of seeing Paullo smile for the first time. It was good to see because when he smiled his face ceased to be that of a worried man and became that of a normal carefree child.

So we have three orphan children with us now. We didn't plan it that way perhaps; but we are happy to have them, and they seem equally delighted to be with us.

I would like to end this chapter concerning "Operation Hanky" and *Maria Pomohwe* on a reflective note. There is so much to do over here, so few to do it, and so little to do it with, that at times one is tempted to become discouraged. Still, one takes solace in the thought that God helps people one at a time, as individuals. We can do no better than to imitate His example.

"Operation Hanky," for example, does not give work to all the needy mothers in Korea. But it does help a significant number in Pusan.

Our family-unit orphanage program will not take care of all the tens of thousands of orphans in Korea. But it will help a significant few, and this is what counts. It is a step, and this is infinitely better than standing idly by gnashing one's teeth and rending one's garments.

PART II

"... *For yours is the Kingdom of Heaven.*"

CHAPTER FOURTEEN

CHRIST LIVES ON in the world today and exerts his influence upon it in three ways: 1) the Eucharist, 2) the inspired word of Scripture, and 3) the person of the poor.

He who made us dwells among us. He can be found not only in the silence of our tabernacles and in the solemn language of our sacred books, but also on our streets and in our marketplaces. The living Christ is as close to us as the nearest poor person.

We see this profound, yet unnamed mystery of the divine indwelling of the poor prepared in the Old Testament. One third of the Psalms revolve about the poverty, affliction, and suffering of men, and the psalmists bring out with lyric tenderness the proximity of God to those in these conditions. The prophets also, the forerunners of Christ, were inspired to associate themselves in a special way with the poor.

Christ, who is the fulfillment and culmination of all that went before, not only associates himself with the poor: He identifies himself with them. Christ proclaimed this truth in a most solemn way in the twenty-fifth chapter of St. Matthew. This passage is considered most important by St. Matthew because he places it at the end of the last of the five great sermons of Christ which form the framework of his entire Gospel. Christ is speaking here of the final judgment and he concludes:

"Then the King will say to those who are on his right hand, 'Come you that have received a blessing from my Father, take possession of the Kingdom which has been prepared for you since the foundation of the world. For I was hungry, and you gave me food, thirsty, and you gave me drink; I was a stranger, and you brought me home, naked, and you clothed me; sick, and you cared for me; a prisoner, and you came to me.' Whereupon the just will answer, 'Lord, when was it that we saw thee hungry, and fed thee, or thirsty, and gave thee drink? When was it that we saw thee a stranger and brought thee home, or naked, and clothed thee? When was it that we saw thee sick or in prison and came to thee?' And the King will answer them, 'Believe me, when you did it to one of the least of my brothers here, you did it to me' "

So now in these last days before the second and final coming of Christ, the poor have been given a new dignity and a new name—and "His name shall be called 'Emmanuel' which is to say 'God-with-us.' "

Down through the history of the Church, the saints, with that penetrating insight and clairvoyance which characterized them, always saw Christ in the person of the poor. In nearly every hagiography one can find an episode in which the saint came into personal contact with Christ through an encounter with a poor man. Whether these stories are woven of fact or fiction matters little. What is important is that they reflect common Christian belief and solid Christian doctrine.

A typical story is that related in the life of St. Martin of Tours. Of a cold wintry night Martin of Tours was returning to Amiens on horseback. A beggar, half-frozen from the cold, asks for alms in the name of Christ. Martin has nothing except his weapons and his clothes, so he rents his cloak in two, gives one half to the beggar, and continues on his way. The following night Christ appears to Martin, clothed in the half-cloak which he gave the beggar, and speaks these words: "Martin, catechumen, has covered me with his garment."

An almost identical episode occurred in the life of St. Catherine of Sienna who exchanged her tunic for the tattered cloak of a beggar. Later in a vision she beheld Christ clothed in this same tunic which is now resplendent with jewels and precious stones.

The saints realized with the greatest clarity possible the "supereminent dignity of the poor" and they felt themselves irresistibly drawn and attracted to them. Blessed Albert of Poland, for example, goes to live among the human derelicts of Warsaw and to minister to them as he would to Christ. A Charles de Foucauld living among the poorest of the poor in the seclusion of the Saharan wastes is another example. In our own day we see a l'Abbé Pierre of Paris seeking out the ragpickers and living among them as if they were royalty. These men of God, searching for God, realize that He is not to be found in the clouds of heaven, but rather in the hovels of the poor.

Of course Christ is not present in the poor in the same manner by which he is present in the Eucharist, or again the same manner by which he is present in Scripture, but it does require the same faith to believe in this presence. It is easier to believe Christ present in an immaculate, richly ornate tabernacle, or to believe him present in the inspired words written on the clean germ-free pages of Scripture, than to believe him present in the unwashed masses of suffering, afflicted, and poverty-stricken humanity.

It requires faith of the deepest kind to see God present in the person of the poor. It requires the faith of the centurion, for example, who could look up at the crushed figure of Christ upon the cross, a figure in whom there was neither beauty nor comeliness, but who was as a leper, as one struck by God, an object of scorn and ridicule, who could look up at this figure and say: "Indeed this was the Son of God."

Or again, the faith of the magi; the three princes who left their pleasure palaces in Persia to follow a star. And the star led them to a stable in Bethlehem where they found a Mother with a newborn Child. The child was wrapped in rags and lying in a manger. The magi fell down adoring and, opening their store of treasure, offered gifts.

The infinite God came to earth to beg two things of man, intellect and will, faith and love. And he wanted these to be given freely, with neither violence nor coercion. The Son of God could have cast himself down unhurt from the pinnacle of the temple and in a blaze of spectacular circus glory forced the belief of all onlookers in the divinity of his person. He also could have fed the crowds with loaves and fishes not once or twice, but every day in order to buy their love.

But God did not want to force belief nor to buy love. He wanted it given in humility and lowliness or he wanted it not at all. It was man's pride of intellect and will which soured and poisoned his relationship with God, and it is this very pride which man must eat and swallow if he is ever to return to God.

So it is that the Infinite God chooses to reveal himself to man through the most finite of finite things: the commonplace, everyday elements of bread and wine, the simple words of human language, a child born in a stable and later nailed to a tree, and the teeming masses of the poor who will always be with us. Man's eyes must be washed with truth and his heart cleansed with humility if he is to come to God on these lowly terms. Such is the inscrutable law of the Incarnation and the pre-ordained economy of salvation.

To a Catholic, faith in the Eucharistic Presence and faith in the divinely inspired character of sacred Scripture comes easily. It is taught him at his mother's knee and he receives it without question. Faith, however, in this yet unnamed presence of Christ in the poor comes much harder. To many, it never comes.

Yet without it, without this union through faith and charity with Christ in the poor, one's Christian life will never attain full stature. In his epistle, St. James writes, "Religion pure and undefiled before God consists in this: to help orphans and widows in their need, and to keep oneself untainted in this world." In other words, if our spiritual life is to swing the full 360-degree arc as intended by God, sooner or later we must come to recognize and embrace Christ in the poor.

It is not sufficient, however, to accept the poor on our terms of human logic and rationalism. We must accept them on God's terms of faith and charity. Otherwise, the poor will always be simply deadbeats, freeloaders, parasites, bums, and beggars. They will never be Jesus of Nazareth.

For instance, consider this:

There is a knock at the rectory door, you open it, and a beggar, hat in hand, eyes downcast, asks for a handout. "You know how it is, Father. Things is tough all over. No work, no money; ain't had nothing to eat since yesterday." You draw back a step, look him up and down, try to get a whiff of his breath to see if he has been drinking, and attempt to trip him up with a sly question or two as he tells his story of hard luck and hard times. Then you try to pass the buck, "How about the Salvation Army, tried them? Or the Red Cross, sometimes they help fellows like you?" He persists. The old squeeze. So you reach down reluctantly in your pocket and give him the dollar, adding to it more than a dollar's worth of free advice. Then you close the door, and with a shrug of the shoulders say, "Well, guess I've been made a sucker of again."

And chances are one has. Not so much by the beggar, however, as by pride and common sense which keep one from seeing and giving to Christ in the poor.

This imaginary episode reminds me of another story told of an English scientist who proudly proclaimed that he would believe in the presence of Christ in the Eucharist only if he were permitted to take a consecrated host from the ciborium, put it on a glass slide, and examine it under a microscope. And, he went on to state, if under the high-powered lens of the microscope he could see some indication of the divinity hidden beneath the bread, then and only then would he believe. If this thing were ever permitted the scientist, all he would see on his little glass slide under his shiny microscope would be the cell formation and chemical compound of bread. Nothing more. He would never see God, for instance.

If we insist, then, on putting the poor on glass slides to examine with high-powered sociology and shiny reason we will seldom see anything of God in them. We must continue to approach them with common sense, yes, but also with something of the beautiful nonsense and utter folly of faith.

Apart from all other considerations, the poor have a definite function in society and an important role to play in the human community. They have been anointed by poverty and suffering to become mediators between man and God. Through them, men are permitted to sacrifice themselves to God, and in turn, God gives himself to men.

Christ's presence in the poor marvelously complements his presence in the Eucharist. In the Sacrament of the Eucharist, the Son of God gives himself to us in the form of bread; and we approach the table of communion as spiritual beggars—with outstretched hand and hungry heart. In the "sacrament of poverty," the roles are mysteriously reversed: Christ is now the beggar, and he humbly approaches us and pleads with us to give him bread.

Just as the Middle Ages were characterized by a general reawakening and deepening of faith in Christ's presence in the Eucharist, so it would seem that our age is called upon by God to develop a greater awareness of Christ's presence in the person of the poor. Although the mode, manner, and means may differ, there is a great similarity between Christ dwelling in the Eucharist and Christ dwelling in the person of the poor. In one case the presence is sacramental, in the other social or mystical. In both cases the presence is real.

◆

CHAPTER FIFTEEN

◆

IN THE PRECEDING chapter the phrase "sacrament of poverty" occurs. The expression is very rich in meaning and I would like to examine it here at greater length. At the same time I would like to treat of a closely related and equally important Gospel idea which may be termed "law of substitution."

Blessed Albert of Warsaw speaks of a "sacrament of poverty" and the phrase occurs also in the writings of Bernanos. The expression, although poetic perhaps, is not without merit from a theological point of view. In more than one sense, poverty may be considered a "natural" sacrament and may be said to possess a certain salvific power.

A sacrament is an outward sign of inward grace, tending to effect that which it signifies. In other words a sacrament tends to accomplish on the inside what it stands for on the outside—*tends*, because God has created man free and God will not violate man's freedom even to sanctify him. Thus, unless man freely consents and cooperates, a sacrament will not accomplish its effect.

The "natural sacrament of poverty" works in a similar manner. Material poverty is normally associated with, stands for, and signifies all that is humble and lowly. Of itself it tends to produce a corresponding inner grace of humility and lowliness. Just as the supernatural sacraments, poverty also does not work automatically, like taking an aspirin for instance. In order that it accomplish on the inside the attitude of humility which it signifies on the outside, poverty must be accompanied by free consent, acceptance, and acquiescence.

If what is said here be true of poverty, the opposite is true of material riches. Material riches tend to produce in the one possessing them an inner attitude of self-satisfaction, complacency, smugness—pride. In the writings of Isaias, Jeremias, and Ezekiel, one frequently comes across the expressions "full belly" and "pride" in the same sentence. The prophets placed these two ideas together because they realized that just as cause follows effect so, too, does pride follow upon material riches and prosperity.

In the Old Testament, we frequently find the prophets turning away from the present prosperity and material ease of the Jews and looking back with longing to the period of the Exodus. During this time the Jews were wanderers on the face of the earth; they were poor and utterly destitute. They were completely dependent on God for their every want and their every need. Their bread was ashes and their wine was mingled with tears. They were stripped of material possessions, security was taken away, and all props were kicked from under them. They were reduced to nothing and were forced to look to the heavens for their nourishment which came down each morning in the form of manna, just enough for that day's needs and no more.

Yet we find the prophets looking back with nostalgia upon this period which the Jewish people spent in the desert. It was a period of truth for the people of Israel, a period when their attitude toward God was most pure, sincere, and humble. It was the period of their deepest poverty and yet it was their finest hour.

A more recent prophet, St. Patrick, perceived with an insight similar to that of the Old Testament prophets how material poverty acts as a preservative upon the moral fiber and religious instincts of a given people. For this reason we find St. Patrick praying a remarkable prayer, namely, that Ireland would always remain poor. If such a prayer were to be uttered in our present day and age, it would be dismissed out of hand as abstract, quietistic, and reactionary. Yet, until recently at least, St.

Patrick's prayer has been heard and Ireland has remained poor. By the same token also, the faith of the Irish people has remained pure and deep, and their religious intuition and fine sense of other-worldliness have, by and large, remained intact.

A person is identified with his possessions, he is one with them, and, in a sense, he *is* what he has. If what a person has, then, is rich, opulent, and magnificent, he tends to look upon himself as someone important and superior.

Following this same psychological pattern, a person's opinion of himself is greatly influenced by what others think of him. If those about one generally look upon him as being successful and important, then he himself easily slips into the inner conviction that he is successful and important. Such is human nature. Our present society, however, is generous in its judgment of people with money. They are considered successful people. The wealthy person, then, upon looking into himself, will usually find there something which causes him, wittingly or unwittingly, to look down upon others less fortunate than himself.

When it comes to poverty, however, this psychological pattern reverses itself. People in society tend to treat the poor with condescension, as individuals who did not make the grade, as persons who are in one respect inferior. Frequently, the poor are even looked down upon, handled with contempt, and treated shabbily. The poor man's opinion of himself will tend to reflect this judgment of society and he will usually end up by thinking of himself in terms which are humble and lowly. Material riches inflate, while poverty cuts one down to his true size before God and men.

In the Gospel, Christ says, "Blessed are the poor, for yours is the kingdom of heaven." He also says, "Unless you first be converted and become as little children you can not enter the kingdom of heaven." In a spiritual sense, a poor man resembles a little child. This is why Christ uses the two terms interchangeably.

A little child is helpless to satisfy his basic needs: he is completely dependent upon his parents and must surrender himself to them in order to survive. Christ tells us that the ideal attitude of man toward God should resemble this attitude of a little child toward his parents. Finite and sinful man must realize that of himself and by himself he is quite helpless to satisfy his most basic spiritual needs. He is absolutely dependent upon God for all that he has and all that he is, in both the natural and supernatural order.

Just as a child depends upon his parents, so, too, does a poor man depend on others for his most basic needs. The poor man is neither self-sufficient, independent, nor secure. He is at the mercy of forces above and outside of himself, and over which he has little control. Just as a little child must look to his parents, so too a poor man must look to Divine Providence to provide him with food for his body and refreshment for his soul.

The only attitude which becomes man—poor, sinful, struggling creature that he is—when he stands before his God is the attitude of the child toward his parents and the poor man toward the world. That is to say, an attitude of utter helplessness, complete dependence, and total surrender. This is the most basic and essential attitude of a finite being in the presence of an Infinite God; yet it is the rarest attitude in the world and the hardest for man to come by.

Man's proud ego is a formidable obstacle on the path to true humility and inner honesty, and few there are who attain it. Poverty, destitution, and insecurity which are not rebelled against bring with them an intense inner experience of one's weakness, helplessness, and nothingness before God; and they leave one washed, cleansed, and humbled.

God resists the proud and gives his grace to the humble. This could not be otherwise because pride is a lie and God loves people too much to encourage them to be liars. This is why Christ speaks so often of poor men and children, why he says: "I have come not for the well, but for the sick. . . . Not for the just, but for sinners. . . . Not for those who see, but for the blind." And this, too, is why St. Paul writes in his first letter to the Corinthians: "Not many of you are wise. . . . Not many powerful, not many well born. No, God has chosen what the world holds foolish. . . . What the world holds weak. . . . What the world holds base and contemptible."

This, too, is why Christ chose twelve poor men to collaborate with him in the world revolution which was launched full sail at the first Pentecost. This is why at Banneux Our Lady refers to herself as "the Virgin of the Poor." And this, too, is one of the reasons why Pope John could say: "The Church of Jesus Christ is the Church of all, but especially the Church of the poor."

A corollary—or at least a closely related idea—to this notion of "sacrament of poverty" is what l'Abbé Jules Monchanin refers to as the "law of substitution." The "law of substitution" means that the measure of poverty and suffering freely accepted in this life reflects the measure of joy to be had in the next life.

The Beatitudes of Christ, as presented in the Lucan Gospel, express very graphically this uneasy doctrine of substitution. In the sixth chapter of St. Luke we read: "Blessed are you who are poor; the kingdom of God is yours. Blessed are you who are hungry now; you will have your fill. Blessed are you who weep now; you will laugh for joy." These words of hope and promise are followed immediately by a solemn warning: "Woe to you rich . . . woe to you who are filled . . . woe to you who laugh now; you shall mourn and weep."

The parable of Lazarus and Dives, as recorded also in St. Luke's Gospel, contains in equally strong and potent language the same doctrine as the Beatitudes. A rich man named Dives, glutton, gourmet, clothed in purple, sits at his banquet table enjoying the good life. Lazarus, poor man, sick man, beggar, stands at the gates of Dives' palace and hungrily watches the dogs eating morsels which fall from his table. The rich man dies. Lazarus dies. The rich man goes to hell and the poor man is carried off by angels to Abraham's bosom to enjoy the wine and roses which were denied him in this life. From the pit of hell a cry is heard. It is the rich man, and he says: "O Father

Abraham, just permit Lazarus to dip his finger in water and with it touch the tip of my tongue to cool it." And back across the chasm of heaven and hell comes the crushing answer: "My child, remember that during your life you have received good things and the poor man here received evil things, now, then he finds his consolation, and you your torture."

Christ was never one to mince his words. His speech was always, "Yes, yes," "No, no"—never "Maybe." So it is that Christ adds nothing to modify this strange doctrine of substitution contained in this story of a have and a have-not. As it stands, the doctrine is a bit disturbing, even unsettling, if, that is, one has the misfortune of being a have. If not, it is a tender song of hope, a soft promise of a new sky and a new earth where the poor will shake off their rags and be clothed in the garments of the Lamb.

Not only the Gospels but the liturgy of the Church as well—especially the feast of the Holy Innocents—remind us of this much-forgotten doctrine of "substitution."

The mystery of the Holy Innocents, whose memory we commemorate the third day after Christmas, is the mystery of all guiltless victims of injustice, from the time of Abel down to the suffering and uncomplaining poor and hungry of our own generation. The feast was celebrated at a very early date by the Church, yet in many ways it is completely unique. These children who have been canonized by the tradition of the Church and who are still venerated as martyrs today did absolutely nothing to earn the titles of saint and martyr. They did nothing except have their heads chopped off as innocent victims of injustice, and they took no active part even in this.

These children were baptized neither by water (the sacrament had not yet been instituted), nor by desire (they had not yet reached the age of reason), nor by blood (they did not freely consent to die for Christ or a Christian principle). They made no acts of faith or love or hope. As I say, they did nothing whatsoever, except to suffer and to die as victims of injustice. Yet God, who alone sanctifies and Who gives his grace when and where he wills, chose such suffering and death to be the instruments of salvation for these children.

The poor of the world, the really poor, are just as much victims of injustice today as were the Holy Innocents. Yet the poor, such as those I have seen in Korea, go one step beyond the Holy Innocents: they—at least passively—consent, accept, and acquiesce to their suffering.

The life of the poor is not severed by one stroke of the tyrant's sword as was the case with the Holy Innocents. Instead it is slowly squeezed out of them by long years of sickness and starvation, ultimately brought about by the failure of the world to accept Christ and his principles. Is it too bold then to go on from here and to say that the poor who do not revolt or rebel, but who inwardly acquiesce to a lifetime of suffering, also should be venerated as saints and martyrs? Is not the name of God, who calls himself "Father of the poor" written on their foreheads also? Are not they of whom St. John writes in his Apocalypse, "They have come from the great tribulation and from their eyes God will wipe every tear"? Like the blood of Abel and that of the Innocents, does not the blood of the shackled poor also cry out to heaven for vengeance? Are not their garments also washed in the Blood of the Lamb?

Writing in the second nocturn of the feast of the Holy Innocents, St. Augustine reduces the whole mystery into one sentence and that not very long. He writes: "In effect, as the most holy solemnity of the present day indicates, in the same measure in which iniquity fell upon these happy children, in that exact same measure has the grace of benediction been poured out upon them." Here St. Augustine seems to be repeating in his own words the mysterious Christian "law of substitution."

It may be argued here that if poverty has a "sacramental" character and if there is such a thing as a "law of substitution," then the poor of the world have a good thing going for them and it may not be a bad idea simply to wish them well and leave them to their sort. This of course is absurd.

Although the "sacrament of poverty" may possess a certain salvific power, of itself and by itself it is incomplete. It must be looked upon merely as a preparation for or a complement to the supernatural sacraments, especially Baptism and the Eucharist, which are the normal channels by which divine life is communicated to men. St. Paul writes: "It is the Will of God that all men be saved and come to knowledge of the truth." The truth is Christ and his Church; and it is the manifest will of God that the poor of the world—and especially the poor—come to a knowledge of these mysteries. Thus, already here below, the poor will be intimately joined to the Mystical Body of Christ and be enabled to participate in the fullness of divine life.

As for the "law of substitution," Christ did not formulate it in order to abandon the poor of the world to their misery and destitution. Rather it serves the twofold purpose 1) of keeping the Lazaruses of the world from going over the brink of despair as they are so often tempted to do, and 2) of encouraging the Dives of the world to take a hard look and think twice about their present easy position.

The Gospels contain an intricately woven and marvelously delicate balance which could have been worked out only by someone who at the same time is both man's Redeemer and his Creator. The Gospels, and the Gospels alone, contain the answer to all the moral and social evils plaguing this parched and poverty-scarred planet of ours.

CHAPTER SIXTEEN

A T THE TIME of Christ, the people of Israel could be divided roughly into four groups: 1) the Pharisees—religious leaders of the Jews, keepers of the Law, lovers of money, self-admirers, holier-than-thou's; 2) the Sadducees—aristocrats, landowners, collaborators with the Roman occupants; 3) the Essenes—ascetic, austere-living, pre-Christian monks; and 4) the People of the Land—the great mass of the unwashed, the have-nots, the poor. Christ chose to associate himself in a special way with the last of these four groups. He was of the people, the unwashed, the have-nots, the poor—and the Sadducees and Pharisees found this very hard to forgive.

There are many elements which group men together and separate them from one another, not the least of which are race and nationality. These factors are physical, easily recognizable, "vertical" traits, so to speak, which classify men into one group or another. There are other characteristics, however, which separate and divide just as radically and drastically as race or nationality. Poverty, for instance.

Poverty, misery, and destitution have at times almost as much impact on the psychology of a given group of people as do race, culture, and nationality. Poverty and hunger have a language which only the poor and hungry can understand. In many respects, a Jew who is poor has more in common with a Greek or Roman who is poor than he has, for example, with another Jew who has never penetrated the world of want and suffering. "Vertically," people are united by race; "horizontally," they are united by common economic and social status.

The infinite, transcendent God thrust himself into the history of man in a special manner on two occasions, each time to make a choice. The first choice was on a "vertical" level. Yahweh selected the sons of Abraham, Isaac, and Jacob, and established a covenant with them: He would be their God, they would be his people. Their descendants would be as numerous as the stars in the heavens and the sands on the seashore, and they would have a future destiny above that of all other peoples.

This first choice, then, was a choice determined by race and blood, a choice of the Jewish people. Within this given race and people, however, God was preparing another, more radical choice which was to be made by his Son and which was to transcend racial and blood lines. This second choice was on a "horizontal" level, a choice of the people of the land, the poor, the humble—and a more startling and revolutionary choice can hardly be imagined. So now, in these last days before the second and final coming of Christ, it is no longer the Jews nor the poor Jews, but the poor, period, who are the chosen people and the elect of God.

Christ's special mission to the disinherited of the earth, his identification with the poor, and his choice of the have-nots, is made crystal clear in the writings of St. Luke, the so-called "social" evangelist.

In the very beginning of Luke's Gospel, there is a detailed account of the episode of the Visitation, in which Mary rises up and goes into the house of Zachary, and salutes Elizabeth. "And Mary said: 'My soul doth magnify the Lord and my spirit hath rejoiced in God, my Saviour.'" A little further on, she continues: "He hath put down the mighty from their seat, and hath exalted the humble. He hath filled the hungry with good things; and the rich he hath sent empty away." In this Canticle of joy, Mary, under the impulse of the Spirit, draws from the purest current of Old Testament religious thought and projects it into the New. In so doing, her words announce ever so softly the breaking of a new dawn for the poor of the earth and they hold forth radiant new hope to the humble and the lowly. It is also interesting to note how the words "proud" and "rich," "humble" and "poor," are juxtaposed in the Magnificat. Mary seems to realize that God has chosen one in preference to the other.

After the episode of the Visitation, St. Luke describes the birth of Christ. In his detailed and colorful description, the following passage is the most significant:

"And there were in the same country shepherds watching . . . over their flock. And behold an angel stood by them . . . and the angel said to them: . . . This day is born to you a Saviour, who is Christ the Lord, in the city of David. And this shall be a sign unto you: You shall find the infant wrapped in swaddling clothes, and laid in a manger."

"And this shall be a sign"—very often the sharp edges of this mystical sign of poverty under which Christ chose to begin his life are softened by the popular representation of the events which took place on that December night in Palestine 2000 years ago. A hundred thousand paintings, drawings, reproductions, and tableaux have effectively done their work; and today, when one thinks of the Nativity, the first thing that comes to mind is a scene almost unbearably charming, picturesque, and sentimental. One sees a chubby, rosy-cheeked, golden-haired child lying on the soft, yellow straw, under a roof of shimmering white snow—and, overhead, the cool silver stars. But a stable is a stable, and by any other name will smell the same; fact is, a stable is a place for animals and as such is dirty, foul-smelling, and unfit for human habitation. And fact is also, it is precisely because a stable lends itself easily as a symbol of extreme poverty that the Son of God chose it as his birthplace, and as the sign by which men would remember His coming.

That Christ was born in a stable is disturbing enough, but after all this might be passed over as just another quirk of history. However, the fact that the event—in sum, *The* event of all time—is first announced to shepherds makes matters even more disturbing. If others were to be brought in on the event as witnesses, one can understand the choice going to kings, statesmen, wise men, men of means and influence; the movers, the builders, the doers, the thinkers, the shapers of world events, those who were something, who counted for something. But shepherds! not only were they poor and uneducated, they were legally unclean as well. Because of their occupation they were unable to fulfill the prescriptions of the law, thus becoming ritually contaminated and, in a sense, social pariahs. Christ, the Son of God, the Expected of Nations, the Awaited of Ages, began his life in poverty and humility and went first to the poor and lowly.

In Chapter Three, St. Luke writes of John the Baptist. He describes him as the "Voice of one crying out in the wilderness." And he tells us that the Voice in the wilderness cried out principally two things: baptism and repentance. When asked what type of repentance, John replied: "He that has two coats, let him give to him that has none; and he that has food let him do in like manner." John's was a fiery, prophetic voice announcing the coming of the Messiah. And in preparation for that coming, he preached social justice and a type of penance directed primarily to the service of the poor.

In Chapter Four of St. Luke, Christ presents himself to us as the New Moses. He shows us that the New Israel of God, the Church, must model itself upon the old Israel in Exodus. As Moses and the people of Israel before Him, Christ, too, is led by the Spirit of God into the desert.

The Jewish people in Exodus were tempted by Satan and fell victim primarily to three types of sin. They worshiped the golden calf, they did not trust God to provide them with food and drink, and they clamored incessantly for signs and wonders.

Christ was confronted by three temptations of a similar nature, temptations which he knew would assail the Church he was about to establish. First, Christ is tempted to change a rock into bread: by resisting this temptation Christ teaches that his kingdom is not a worldly kingdom of eating and drinking, but a spiritual one of prayer and fasting. Secondly, Christ is tempted by wealth and riches: by repelling this temptation Christ teaches that his kingdom is not a kingdom of money and prosperity, but of poverty and renunciation. Lastly, Christ is tempted to cast himself down unharmed from the temple so that the people gathered below might believe in him: by turning aside this temptation Christ teaches that he does not wish to force men to believe in him through spectacular signs and wonders, but wishes faith to be given freely, in humility and lowliness.

All three synoptic Gospels record the episode of Christ's temptations, and the question subsequently comes to mind: How did they know about it? Other than the three principals themselves, Christ, Satan, and the angels, there were no witnesses; yet both Matthew and Luke describe the event in detail and Mark at least makes mention of it. One is led to assume that Christ himself related the episode to his apostles because, occurring as it did just before the beginning of his public ministry, it was of great importance in shedding light on the nature of the Church he had come to establish.

Following the account of the temptations, St. Luke describes the beginning of Christ's public ministry in Galilee. Christ, on a visit to his home town of Nazareth, enters the synagogue for the Sabbath service. As is the custom at times, Christ stood up to read. The Book of Isaias the prophet is brought unto him. He unfolds it, searches, finds the place he is looking for, then slowly and solemnly begins to read: "The spirit of the Lord is upon me, wherefore he has anointed me to preach the gospel to the poor." In the Gospel of St. Luke these words represent the very first public pronouncement of the Messiah. As such they are of utmost importance. The significance of the gesture is unmistakable, its meaning clear: Christ has come primarily for the poor and the Church he was about to establish would be primarily a Church of the poor.

A little later, but still in the beginning of Christ's ministry in which the great lines of his messianic approach were being drawn up, St. Luke recounts another episode in which this same citation from Isaias figures prominently.

John the Baptist, imprisoned in Herod's palace, sends two of his followers to question Christ as to whether or not he is the Messiah. John himself is not too sure of the answer. It would seem that he had expected, even hoped for, someone a little different in the way of a Messiah, someone a little more fiery and vengeful. The disciples of John, then, dutifully seek out Christ and begin their interrogation: Are you the one who is to come? Or should we look for another? Christ tells them to return to the one who had sent them and report exactly what they had seen, to wit: the dumb speak, the deaf hear, the blind see, the lame walk, the lepers are cleansed, the dead rise, and the poor have the Gospel preached to them.

The disciples of John knew Isaias had foretold that the Messiah would heal the sick, raise the dead, and preach the Gospel to the poor. Christ was doing just that and he points to the fact as proof of the authenticity of his messianic mission. Such were his credentials, and one assumes that the disciples of John went away convinced.

If the disciples of John the Baptist were to return to earth today, they would ask of the Church the same series of questions that they asked of Christ 2000 years ago in order to establish his authenticity. Are you the one who is to come? Or should we look for another? Are you the City of God, the New Jerusalem, the Expected of the Nations? Or should we go elsewhere?

In reply, the Church would say: See for yourself, the poor of the world have the Gospel preached to them.

And the disciples of John would answer: Do they?

Statistically, the evidence is to the contrary. The poor of the world—at least eighty-five per cent of them—are in Africa, Asia, and South America, while eighty-five per cent of those commissioned by God to announce the Gospels to them—priests, brothers, and sisters—are elsewhere. They are mostly in America and Europe where the land is fat and the people who dwell therein rich. Can it really be said, then, that there is a massive, concerted, selective effort on the part of the Church today to seek out the poor of the world and to bring them the message of salvation?

Furthermore, since an army, albeit a spiritual one, marches on its stomach, can it be said also that there is a mounted program on the part of the Church today to support fully the Church's divinely received, world-wide mission to the poverty-stricken? Once again, the evidence indicates that such is not the case. To give but one slim example: in a year when the Society for the Propagation of the Faith in the United States collects only $13,000,000 for support of the Church's world-wide mission effort, dioceses such as New York and Brooklyn effortlessly raise $35,000,000 and $45,000,000 respectively for their own local building programs. The rich churches get richer and the poor churches continue to get the crumbs.

Oversimplified? Perhaps. Yet nothing is quite so simple and straightforward as the words of Christ when taken at face value. No hemming or hawing; no qualifying or modifying; no if, but, or maybe; just "the poor have the gospel preached to them," period.

This relentless theme of God's choice of the poor occurs again in the fourteenth chapter of St. Luke, this time in parable form. The story concerns a certain man who made a great supper and invited many guests. When everything was in readiness, the servant of this certain man went out gaily to bring in those who had been invited, only to discover that they all had made other plans. One had bought a farm, another a yoke of oxen, one had married a wife. All hoped that the master of the house would understand and they prayed to be held excused. But the master did not understand and he did not hold them excused. Instead he got very angry and he said to his servant: "Go out quickly into the streets and lanes of the city and bring in hither the poor and the feeble, and the blind and the lame."

St. James expresses a similar idea in different words when he writes in the second chapter of his epistle: "Harken, my dearest brethren: hath not God chosen the poor in this world, rich in faith, and heirs to the kingdom which God has promised to them that love him."

In reading St. Luke and other inspired writers—especially St. Paul and St. James—it becomes quite clear that the Church's primary mission is to preach the Gospel to the poor of the world. These constitute the only true "elite," in the Christian acceptance of the term. As for the Church's apostolate to the rich and powerful, this should in no way be neglected, but it should always be in reference to the poor. That is, the Church administers to the rich and powerful in order to make them aware of their responsibility to the poverty-stricken and in order to encourage them to use their power and wealth in the service of the poor.

The Church must not only be able to say of itself, as did Christ, its Founder, "He has anointed me to announce the gospel to the poor," but also, "Learn of me for I am poor and humble of heart."

The Church is the Mystical Body of Christ, the Bride of Christ, another Christ. The Church is a projection of the living Christ into time and space. She is a sacrament and a sign and, as such, points to a reality other than herself. This reality is the Christ of Bethlehem and Calvary who came in poverty and rags and left in defeat and humiliation.

Those who study the face of the Church and seek out the secrets of her heart must come away with the knowledge of the face and heart of Christ. Otherwise the Church has betrayed her mission and is no longer sacrament and sign. The face of Christ, however, as portrayed by the prophets and evangelists, is the face of a poor man, a servant, and a slave. The heart of Christ, as presented by these same writers, is the heart of one who is poor and lowly. So, too, must be the heart and face of the Church.

In the early centuries of Christendom, the fifty-third chapter of Isaias, in which Christ is described as one in whom there is neither beauty nor comeliness, had such influence in shaping Christian thought that in certain circles it gave rise to the belief that the historical Christ was a hunchback or a leper, that is, one who was humiliated by God by physical deformity. Although certainly inaccurate, this belief is based upon sound theology and is not without merit. Christ came the first time in poverty, humility, and abjection, because of which God, the Father, raised him up, glorified him, and gave him a name which is above every name. Since the servant is not above his master, the Church, too, is subject to the same economy of salvation and the same law of redemption. That is, she too must freely accept and submit to poverty, humility, and abjection in order to participate in Christ's glorification and triumph.

St. John, in his Gospel, frequently contrasts the glory of God with the glory of men. The two are not to be confused, for not only are they not the same, but they are diametrically opposed. The glory of men is found in riches, success, power, and being well thought of. When God, however, seeks his glory among the children of men, he goes looking for it in a stable in a little town not far from Jerusalem, and again on a cross planted on a hill just outside that same city. At Bethlehem the angels sang, "Glory to God in the highest," because the Son of God was wrapped in swaddling clothes and lying in a manger. Again, Christ on several occasions refers to the mystery of Calvary in similarly exalted language, e.g., "The hour of the glorification of the Son of man is at hand."

One must bear in mind that Bethlehem and Calvary are not two different realities, but essentially one and the same mystery. Calvary is the consummation of that same sacrifice which began at Bethlehem, which continued throughout the life of Christ, and which is basically a sacrifice of absolute obedience to the Father expressed in freely accepted poverty, humiliation, and suffering.

St. Paul in his first letter to the Corinthians goes right to the heart of this double mystery and argues eloquently that the Church, according to the mind of Christ, must always be clothed in weakness and foolishness. St. Paul writes:

> For both the Jews require signs, and the Greeks seek after wisdom: but we preach Christ crucified, unto the Jews indeed a stumbling block, and unto the Gentiles foolishness: but unto them that are called, both Jews and Greeks, Christ the power of God, and the wisdom of God. For the foolishness of God is wiser than men; and the weakness of God is stronger than men. . . . But the foolish things of the world hath God chosen, that he may confound the wise; and the weak things of the world hath God chosen, that he may confound the strong. And the base things of the world, and the things that are contemptible, hath God chosen, and things that are not, that he might bring to nought things that are. . . .

The Jews and the Greeks of the twentieth century still require the same signs, still seek after the same wisdom. For such as these, the Church, by her poverty, humility, and lowliness, must always remain a scandal and a stumbling block. The Church, according to the mind of Christ, must always incarnate in its members the mystery of Calvary and Bethlehem. And what is equally important, this mystery must always shine forth and be immediately apparent to all observers. Otherwise, the Church is no longer sacrament and sign and a light shining forth for all to see. What is more, those who seek in her the glory of men will find it, and those who seek the glory of God will be troubled and dismayed. By building her strength on the weakness of Bethlehem and her wisdom on the foolishness of Calvary, the Church will fulfill her divine mission of being an eternal sign of contradiction.

In St. Luke's Gospel, when Christ was replying to the disciples of John, immediately after the statement, "The poor have the Gospel preached to them," Christ added, "And blessed is he who shall not be scandalized in me." Blessed also is he who will not be scandalized by a Church which ministers primarily to the poor and which bears in its members the marks of Bethlehem and Calvary.

Certainly many people will be scandalized and will be repelled by such a Church: the type of person, for instance, who rushed to make Christ king only after he had filled his belly with the loaves and fishes; the type who would have believed in Christ only if he had heeded the devil's suggestion to cast himself down unharmed from the temple; the type who looked up at Christ on Golgotha and scoffed, "If you be the Son of God, come down that we may believe in you." In the Book of Wisdom, however, it is written: "Let those who are little ones come unto me." Those who are truly little ones, therefore, will not be turned away by a Church of poverty and a Church of the poor. On the contrary, they will be drawn by the secret action of the Spirit to believe in her and to embrace her.

Almost from her inception the Church has been plagued by the evil of material riches. As early as the third century, in the writings of Pastor Hermes, one sees the Church compared to an old lady seated in an easy chair, well fed, well heeled, and well satisfied. In the thirteenth century Francis of Assisi was told by Christ to rebuild his then-crumbling Church, and the principal tool to be used in this reconstruction was poverty. Again in the sixteenth century the assembled bishops and cardinals at Trent agreed that the greatest evil infecting the Church at that time was the evil of material riches. And today? There are voices today both in the mission world and the mission-sending world which say the same thing. And they say it with conviction and factual evidence which is not to be denied.

One day, so the story goes, St. Dominic was being shown around the city of Rome by the reigning sovereign pontiff. After conducting the saint through the city and pointing out all the pomp, splendor, and riches of Renaissance Rome, the pope turned to his guest and said, "The Church can no longer say as did St. Peter in the Acts of the Apostles, 'Gold and silver I have not.'" St. Dominic replied: "By the same token the Church can no longer say, 'Take up thy crutch and walk.'"

A poverty-inspired Church which goes primarily to the poor is a Church of miracles, a Church according to the mind of Christ. A prestige-conscious Church, heavy with wealth and overly interested in the rich, is a Church which has lost its élan and is as salt which has lost its savor.

CHAPTER SEVENTEEN

THERE ARE MANY liberating truths in the Gospels. Among the most effective of these are those which treat of material riches and poverty. In these truths the disciple of Christ finds his personal Magna Carta, Declaration of Independence, and Bill of Rights all rolled into one.

For instance, the simple and sublime statement that the poor are blessed shows one how to escape from the financial rat race and indicates with marvelous accuracy the direction in which the "freedom of the glory of the sons of God" is to be found. Most people go through life bent over under the weight of daily, all-consuming material care and worry. The axis about which their lives turn are the questions: What shall I have for supper tonight? What shall I serve my friends at the party next week? What shall I wear to church on Sunday? Christ, the Liberator, says to these people: "Do not be concerned about what you shall eat, or drink, or put on . . . but seek first the Kingdom of Heaven and all the rest shall be given you."

Christ goes on to say that he who hates his life in this world shall find it, and that he who renounces all that he possesses shall find true happiness. These and similar divinely revealed truths breathe that sweet, soft air of spiritual freedom which is promised the children of light.

God is simplicity. His existence and essence are one. God possesses nothing, has nothing: He is. The more one moves, then, in the direction of God, the more simple and uncomplicated must one's life become. A movement toward the uncreated God implies a concomitant movement away from created things. In order to explore the marvelous world of the Trinity which dwells within one, one must break free of the gravitational pull of the earth and become as weightless as an astronaut sailing on the seas of outer space.

Material wealth exerts a power over those who possess it and this power must be definitively broken if one wishes to possess Christ. No one can be a slave to material riches and still call himself a disciple of Christ.

The words freedom, liberty, independence are very popular in Western society and are bandied about quite a bit. These terms are usually employed, however, to refer to political and economic freedom, which is to say freedom at its most shallow and superficial level. The freedom of Christ is quite different. This freedom penetrates the heart of man and is a deeply liberating inner experience which makes one throw out his arms and lift up his face to the open sky and laugh for joy. Such as did "the little poor man" of Assisi, who remains for all time the classic example of Christian poverty.

Every word of St. Francis's beautiful canticle to the sun is informed by this Christian freedom, which in truth can be found only in poverty. St. Francis pushed the doctrine of Christian poverty to the very limits of human resistance and little by little he experienced its marvelously liberating effects, until finally he could sing and shout, as free as a child, reaching out to embrace all creation and call it his own. "For all things are yours, and you are Christ's, and Christ is God's."

St. Paul, as perhaps no one before him and few people after him, was passionately addicted to personal freedom and intensely fond of intellectual liberty. It is only natural, then, that it was he who captured once and for all the freshness and spontaneity of Christian poverty when he wrote that beautiful autobiographical sentence: "I know how to live in abundance and I know how to live in want."

The essence of Christian poverty, as suggested in the

previous sentence, consists mainly in a basic, far-reaching, all-embracing independence from material things. There is a saying in French which when translated reads something like this: "A monk may have only a nail in his cell but he still can become attached to it."

It is not so much, then, a question of how much or how little one possesses, but rather how detached and how free one is from his possessions. It is necessary to add immediately, however, that detachment, freedom, and independence from material things run the risk of being wishful thinking and mere figments of the imagination until they have been tried, tested, and tempered in the fire and water of real, belt-tightening, physical poverty. It is difficult to approach the heart and center of Christian poverty and to discover its hidden promise of spiritual freedom while one is living in the lap of luxury. It can be done—I am not saying the contrary—but it's something extremely difficult to achieve in this flesh-and-blood world of ours.

Who says Christian poverty says Christian freedom. The next question which arises then, and a very vital one, is: Why do I wish to be free?

For instance, consider the Buddhist mystics. Not the deadbeats nor the charlatans, but the real ones. They, too, wish to be free, and to achieve this freedom they assume an ideal of poverty. Clothed in saffron robes, heads shaved, eyes closed, legs crossed, they sit on the bare floors of their temples and swaying back and forth they recite their "Ninety-nine desires, ninety-nine sorrows" litany. The goal which they set for themselves in life is freedom from all desire of created possessions in order to arrive at a state of inner nothingness, called *Nirvana*. The disciple of Buddha wishes to be free in order to enjoy a tranquil existence far removed from the enslaving bother and care of material wealth. Is it for a similar motive that the disciple of Christ wishes to be free? Or is it for something a little better?

Then, too, consider the Stoics of ancient Greece. They also

sought a type of freedom through poverty. The renunciation of the Stoics, although not oriented toward Nirvana, was aimed at something akin to it called *apatheia*. They wished to lead a peaceful and comfortable life, intellectually and emotionally undisturbed by the trials and vicissitudes which accompany material wealth. Is it for this that the Christian wishes to be free? Or is it for something a little higher?

The answer to the preceding questions is to be found in the thirteenth chapter of St. Paul's first letter to the Corinthians: "If I give all my goods to the poor and have not charity it profits me nothing." In other words, St. Paul is saying here that Christian poverty, unlike that of the Buddhists and the Stoics, is neither negative, egocentric, nor self-centered: it is essentially positive, alterocentric, Christo-centric, theocentric. Christian poverty tends to take one out and away from self toward God, existing in his own Person and existing in one's neighbor.

In the golden light of St. Paul's chapter on charity, poverty is clearly seen to be a means and not an end. Poverty is the servant, charity the queen. Yet the two, poverty and charity, are so clearly linked together that a consideration of one necessarily entails a consideration of the other and any disassociation of the two risks distorting them.

Here it is well to note that there is just one love, one charity, in the world: the love of man for God rejoins and dissolves in the love of man for man. If I wish to know how much do I love God, I simply ask the question, how much do I love my neighbor? Love of neighbor is an unerring thermometer by which the Christian measures the degree of intensity of his love of God. "For if any man says that he loves God whom he does not see, and hates his neighbor whom he sees, that man is a liar."

And who is my neighbor? This question was first asked some 2000 years ago in Palestine. The one asking was a certain lawyer who, tempting Christ, began with the most vital question ever asked in the history of the world: "What must I do to possess eternal life?" From there he was led to ask for a definition of the term "neighbor." The one answering, of course, was Christ, and he said: "A certain man went down from Jerusalem to Jericho. . . ." In the parable of the Good Samaritan which followed, Christ gives a good definition of the word "neighbor," whom one must love in order to achieve eternal life.

Christ chose a Samaritan and a Jew as the principals of the parable, with the role of hero going to the Samaritan. The Samaritans were as different from the Jews as night from day. Moreover, they cordially and warmly hated each other. In this parable, the Jew is contrasted with the Samaritan and as such represents the stranger and the foreigner. He is the symbol of everyone whose skin and tongue is different from mine, of him who lives across the waters and beyond the seas. He is my neighbor and my brother, and his name is Everyman.

The implications of the parable are overwhelming and staggering. In effect, Christ is telling us that if at present there are three billion five hundred million people in the world, then my neighbor and my brother and he whom I must love in order to attain eternal life is three billion five hundred million minus one. So much then for whom I must love.

The second question is: How must I love? The answer to this question, as contained in the Gospels, is just as broad and sweeping as the answer to the first. If my neighbor and my brother is Everyman, then I must love him in Everyway.

In his first epistle, St. John writes:

> In this we have known the charity of God that he laid down his life for us. We ought to lay down our life for the brethren. He who has the goods of this world and sees his brother in need and closes his heart to him, how can you say the love of God is in you. My little children, let us not love in word and in tongue, but in truth and in action.

St. John has been called the mystic writer, the Eagle, and at times, borne on the wings of the Spirit, he soars to transcendent spiritual heights. At the same time, however, as seen in the above passage, his two feet are solidly planted on mother earth and he is firmly rooted in reality. In effect, St. John is saying that love of neighbor does not consist in pious feelings of togetherness or lovely words about the brotherhood of men, but in doing and in giving. Love is effectively expressed only in action and effectively proven only in doing.

One must be willing to lay down his life for the brethren. This does not mean (although it does not exclude it either) that all one has to do is to sit patiently at his banquet table and to wait for the glory of martyrdom to be presented him as his own severed head upon a silver platter.

Implied in St. John's words is a psychological fact which I have mentioned previously, namely: the fact that man tends to be identified with what he has and he is one with what he possesses. When man gives of his possessions he is giving of himself and when one distributes what he has to his neighbor he is, in effect, laying down his life for his brother.

So, looking around at the three billion five hundred million people minus one in the world who are included in the terms neighbor and brother, I see at present that he is in desperate need. In Hong Kong he is homeless, in Korea he is jobless, in India he is sick, in South America he is hungry, in Africa he is uneducated. Just as Christ, then, laid down his life for me, so I, too, must lay down my life for my neighbor. I must give of myself in the form of my possessions.

By possessions, however, I do not mean the old clothes in my attic nor the newspapers in the basement, nor the canceled stamps in my desk drawer. I mean mostly money. Nothing is so quickly given, so rapidly transferred, and represents such immediate power to transform hunger into contentment, sickness into health, ignorance into knowledge, and unemployment into jobs as that everyday, much maligned, much abused, vulgar substance—money. It has been called many things; everything from "excrement of the devil" to "filthy lucre." Yet it talks. It can speak the language of Christian love, and it speaks it most eloquently, dramatically, and forcefully.

It is clear, then, that poverty and charity are intimately bound together and that it is very difficult really to love without letting one's possessions get away from him. The world situation being what it is and the laws of Christian charity being what they are, if one really loves one will inevitably become, if not downright poor himself, at least considerably poorer.

St. John tells us that God loved us first. Now it is our turn to return this charity by loving God in himself and in our neighbor. Using much the same logic, St. Paul tells us that Christ was poor first. Now we must reciprocate. Christ, in the person of the poor, will endure poverty and misery until the end of time. If I am rich in the goods of this world, then I must dispossess myself and become poor in order that the lot of Christ, the Eternal Poorman, may be made a little easier.

Some people object—and object vehemently—that the giving of one's possessions (mostly in the form of money) is at best an impractical solution to the problem of world poverty. They argue that until international social-economic structures are changed it is futile to do anything. They feel that if they were to follow Christ's command to give their goods to the poor it would be merely an insignificant drop in the bottomless bucket of world poverty and would not change anything. They are convinced that their personal, individual charity to the poor would do little or nothing to alter the directions of lives. As a matter of fact, they dismiss the whole issue with a shrug of the shoulders and the offhand remark: "What good would it do?"

Before attempting to reply to the above objections, it is important to note that two questions are involved here: 1) Christian poverty, and 2) Christian charity to the poor. Granted that the two are inter-related, nonetheless, for purposes of clarification, it is necessary to distinguish. Christian poverty needs no justification other than the fact that Christ

himself was poor, is poor (in the person of the world's hungry
and needy), and will continue to be poor ("The poor you will
always have with you") until his ultimate triumph at the end
of time. Thus, the principal arguments for Christian poverty
are drawn from the supernatural order of faith and charity
—an order which certainly does not contradict, but which does
go considerably beyond, the purely natural order of reason,
logic, and simple practicality.

In reference to Christian charity to the poor and in answer
to the above question, "What good would it do?"—it would
do immeasurable good first and foremost to the one practicing
it. The adage, "It is more blessed to give than to receive," did
not originate on Madison Avenue; it is a divinely revealed
truth first uttered by Christ himself.

Almsgiving offers so many rich spiritual benefits to the individual practicing it that in many ways it resembles the sacrament of confession. Sacred Scripture movingly and mysteriously describes charity to the poor in terms of a spiritual
catharsis. For example: "As fire quenches water so does almsgiving take away sin" (Book of Ecclesiastes). "If you would
be clean on the inside, give alms of all that you possess" (St.
Luke). "Charity covers a multitude of sins" (St. Paul). And
so on. Charity to the poor not only atones for sin: it even takes
away sin and helps achieve inner purity.

What good would charity to the poor do to the one receiving? Would it alter lives and change the direction of human
existence? The answer to these questions is an emphatic "yes."
In the Third World of hunger, where average annual income
ranges in the $100 bracket, an isolated donation of ten dollars,
say, can profoundly influence human life. Continued on a
regular basis, such a donation can permanently and radically
alter it.

Let me illustrate my point with a few examples taken from
my own parish here in Pusan.

Agatha Han: age forty-one, widow, suffering from stomach
cancer, four small children, no income, no means of support;

wants letter of recommendation from pastor in order to place children in an orphanage. Ten dollars a month will prevent this and enable this family to survive as a family. A gift of this amount, then, is all that would be needed to change permanently the direction of life of an entire family.

Cho Il Sun: thirty-two, blind, beggar, lives with wife and younger brother and sister in makeshift shanty near here; wants a loan of twenty-five dollars to enable him and his wife to set up a clothing stall in Pusan market. The income from this enterprise, although small, would permit him and his family to live more or less as human beings instead of as undernourished animals.

Pak U Taek: seventeen, parentless, shoe-shine boy, lives in cave, losing his hearing; asks for fifty dollars to pay for ear operation at Bundo Hospital. Doctor says that operation will not only relieve the pain of his ear affliction but will also save his hearing.

Lee Veronica: forty-seven, lives with husband and five children; two remaining children sleep in neighbors' houses because there is not enough room in her hut for the whole family to lie down on the floor at the same time; requests loan of forty dollars to build new and larger shanty. A gift of this nature will radically alter her life and that of her husband and children.

One can draw up an almost inexhaustible list of similar examples, but it is not necessary. The point is, charity to the poor as practiced by an individual American to another individual who is a citizen of the Third World of hunger can effect profound and lasting good and can permanently alter the course of human life.

Another question which sometimes arises is, how should one give? At present there are more than 7000 American priests, brothers, sisters, and lay missioners serving in Africa, Asia, and South America. One could channel his gift to the poor through any one of these, or their representatives in the United States. Or through Catholic Relief Services, or the Society for the Propagation of the Faith. Or, for that matter, through any one of the hundreds of American voluntary relief agencies now working overseas. This question does not merit undue attention. Once one is convinced of the need to give and is possessed of a will to give, a way to give will be easily found.

As was mentioned above, some people think that because they can do little to change the world of poverty as such, or to lift up the mass of the poor as a mass, they are relieved of responsibility to do anything on a person-to-person basis. This is blatantly false. Christ does not indwell the masses of the poor as a group or a collectivity; on the contrary, he is present in the heart of each individual poor person. Christ did not say, "As long as you do it to *these* . . . ," but, "As long as you do it to *one* of these, the least of my brethren, you do it to me." It is not necessary to assist the multitude of the poor as a multitude for Christ to take notice: it is enough to help them one at a time.

The person who reasons that it is necessary to help all—or none—may be likened to the person in the following example. A man with a lifebelt in his hand is standing on the shore of a storm-driven sea in which a billion people are struggling for survival. Overwhelmed by the knowledge that he cannot save the entire billion, or even a significant fraction thereof, the man drops his lifebelt, turns his back on the sea of drowning individuals, and decides to wait. He decides to wait until the heads of state and the spiritual leaders devise a master plan to dry up the sea and permit the entire billion people to walk safely to shore.

Another way of phrasing the preceding objection is by saying that until international social-economic institutions are changed it is futile to help on an individual basis. Before social structures and institutions can be changed, however, there must be a transformation of individual mentality. This would seem to be the Christian view of things. Christ, for example, never preached: "*Nations*, love each other." But rather: "Love *thy* neighbor."

Christ was not bent so much on changing social-economic structures *per se*, as he was on changing the mentality of individuals. Take but one example—human slavery. At the time of Christ, slavery was a flourishing institution, yet neither Christ nor his apostles hit it head on. Instead, Christ and his apostles worked at changing individual hearts and minds until finally, after two or three centuries, the walls of slavery came tumbling down. Economic slavery today is just as degrading, crippling, and stultifying as the institution of human slavery at the time of St. Paul. Its change, too, will be brought about only through the transformation of individual mentalities, and this is possible only through charity.

In the Canticle of Canticles it is written: "Charity is strong as death. . . . It is like a flame, the flame of Yahweh. Mighty waters will not quench it nor will rivers submerge it." And in the epistle of St. John one reads: "He who abides in charity, abides in God and God in him." Charity is a divine, infinitely potent force which is at man's disposal. Charity—and charity alone—has the power to transform the world and renew the face of the earth.

CHAPTER EIGHTEEN

O H POVERTY OF SPIRIT, what crimes are committed in thy name! The revelation of Christ concerning the evil of material riches is forthright and explicit and there is little room for misunderstanding. Yet one finds the clear strong wine of this doctrine frequently diluted with vague and watery references to poverty of spirit. The resulting mixture, tasteless and insipid, goes down as effortlessly as a long drink of water and is far removed indeed from the rich, heady stuff which nourished and inspired the lives of the saints.

It is difficult to possess deep supernatural faith and charity without at the same time being driven by these inner, spiritual forces to embrace a life of real material poverty. Nor is it possible to adhere totally to the living Christ and at the same time reject in part his doctrine concerning poverty. The part rejected, moreover, is always the part concerning material poverty. There is little difficulty with poverty of spirit: everyone seems agreed that this is a good thing. It is a different story, however, when it comes to material poverty. Few there are who consider material poverty an authentic Christian value; and fewer still those who look upon it as something to be desired and sought after, something even necessary and indispensable for the full Christian life. Yet the arguments which indicate that such is so are strong and compelling. And they are many.

First is the argument based upon charity. If I love as God loves me, and as Christ commands me to love, I can hardly remain indifferent to the poverty and suffering in the world.

Sooner or later I will be moved to do something about it, and there is nothing quite so direct and essentially Christian to do about it as the giving of one's possessions.

The importance and necessity of giving are stressed in writings of both the Old and the New Testament. In the twelfth chapter of the Book of Tobias, for instance, we read that prayer, when accompanied by fasting and alms, is most acceptable and pleasing to God: "For alms delivers from death and the same is that which purges away sins and makes to find mercy and life everlasting." Christ expresses this same Old Testamentary idea in the New Testament when he turns on the Pharisees and says: "If you wish to be clean on the inside sell what you possess and give alms to the poor."

Upon reading these and similar words of Christ, the question comes to mind: To what extent must I give? Is one tenth enough? Or must I give half of my possessions as did Zacheus in the Gospel story? Or perhaps does Christ demand all as he did of the rich young man in the Gospel of St. Mark? This ultimately is for each to decide in the forum of his own conscience; nevertheless, one practical rule of thumb may be of some help here.

As one's wealth increases, his standard of living should remain more or less the same. At the same time, the standard of living of Christ in the person of the poor should considerably improve. More money does not mean more personal pleasure, security, and prestige. It means simply that one now has more to give to Christ in the poor, and more to invest in eternal happiness.

For example: a young couple starts off in life—not with a plush, ranch-style, split-level residence in some suburban area —but with a modest six-room house in a poor section of town. Furnishings include necessities, but they do not include: stereo, electric dishwasher, deep freeze, air conditioner, wall-to-wall carpeting, et al. For transportation, the young couple use a Volks. Food, although wholesome and adequate, is mostly of the hamburger, meat-loaf variety. As time goes by, promotions come, wages increase, more money flows in. But—except for necessary minor adjustments—the basic standard of living of the couple does not change. The standard of living, however, of a poor family in Pusan and another in Calcutta does. It changes radically and permanently: these families are now able to eat, and to be clothed and sheltered as human beings rather than as animals. At the same time, the temporal health and happiness of the young couple in the example are in no way affected. Their eternal health and happiness, however, are immensely affected—to the good, of course.

St. Paul in his writings tells us that the disciple of Christ should aspire after the simple life and tend to eliminate as much as possible frills, extras, and luxuries. For example, in Timothy 6:7–8, we read: "For we brought nothing into this world and certainly we can carry nothing out. But having food and wherewith to be covered, with these we are content."

But who is to be judge of what is luxury and what is necessity? The poor of the world—that's who. In the twenty-fifth chapter of St. Matthew, Christ places the verdict of our final judgment in the hands of the poor. If this be the case, then, we should get in the habit now of submitting every decision of the luxury-necessity type to the ruthless scrutiny and examination of the poor. A pleasure trip to Europe, a new boat, an expensive pet, a new permanent—luxury or necessity? The answer: How would a person who is poverty-stricken, hungry, and destitute look upon it? This is the only objective norm, and, in sum, it is the criterion of Christ himself.

If I am really convinced that Christ lives on in the poor of the world—and how can I be otherwise and still call myself Christian?—if I am really convinced of this, then I must become like Christ in the poor. One of the purest expressions and highest forms of love is identification and conformity with the one loved. If my love of Christ is real and effective, I must identify myself with Christ in the poor and I must establish solidarity with him by becoming poor myself, not only spiritually but materially as well.

Along these same lines, if one is really in love, he is willing not only to climb the highest mountain and swim the deepest ocean, but, what is more difficult, he is willing to change his habits and tastes to please the one he loves. For example, if the person one loves is allergic to cigarette smoke, one should be willing to give up smoking, or if he cannot stand the sight of someone chewing gum, one should be willing to foreswear the pleasure of gum-chewing. And so on. But God, it would seem, is somewhat allergic to and turns away from material riches. In the Gospel of St. Luke, following the Dives-Lazarus parable, Christ has this to say in reference to material riches and money: "What is held up in the eyes of men God holds in abomination." In order to please God, therefore, one should be willing to turn away as much as possible from that which he holds in abomination.

Not only will charity, if it be deep, intense, and authentic, lead one to imitate Christ in his poverty, but faith also leads one in this direction. If one believes in Christ, who was manifestly poor, one must also believe in the necessity of imitating him: "An example have I given you, as I have done so must you do also." And: "If you abide in him, you must walk as he walked."

It is important to note that Christian poverty is founded first upon faith in Christ and not upon faith in man, that it is based primarily upon love of the Son of God and only secondarily upon love of one's fellow man. The supreme and ultimate justification of Christian poverty springs not from reasons of a practical or utilitarian order, but from reasons of a supernatural order, founded on faith and charity. These reasons are a desire to imitate Christ, to live as he lived, to walk as he walked—and in so doing become united and identified with him. Suppose, for the sake of argument, that one sold all his goods but there were no poor left in the world to give them to—then what? Suppose, also, that one wished to give alms of all that he possessed but there was no longer anyone on the planet who needed, or even wanted, alms—then what? Suppose, again, one wished to leave all things to follow Christ but could find no one to leave them to—what then?

If these contrary-to-fact conditions were ever to be realized, then the disciple of Christ would still be no less obliged to live a life of poverty. Why? Because Christ, the Lord and Master, was poor, and this reason overshadows every other consideration. Any ideal less than imitation of Christ is unworthy of one who claims to be his follower; and, any imitation of Christ without his poverty is misguided make-believe. Why Christ in his incomprehensible folly and weakness chose poverty for his constant companion is another question. The fact that he did so is incontrovertible; and, for the Christian, there is no escaping its implications.

Moreover, faith, not only in the Person of Christ, but in his words and teachings as well, should induce one slowly but surely to believe in the necessity of some form of material poverty, absolute or modified, in order to lead a full Christian life.

It is perplexing how people will read, retain, and repeat what St. Matthew has to say about poverty and yet never give St. Luke a glance. Yet these two writers, St. Matthew and St. Luke, complement each other and when taken together they present the revelation of Christ on the subject in its full scope and totality. Here, no doubt, the Scripture scholar will protest that Matthew's is the more primitive of the two Gospels and the words recorded in his Gospel are the more authentic. Granted. Yet both Matthew and Luke are equally inspired and both contain in equal degree the revelation of Christ, however much they may differ in nuance, emphasis, and perspective.

St. Matthew writes: "Blessed are the poor in spirit." He means blessed are the humble, the meek, the lowly, those who are detached from material things and adhere only to the eternal God.

St. Luke writes: "Blessed are the poor." Period. Not "poor in spirit," just "poor." He means blessed are those who have renounced material riches and who live lives of down-to-earth, concrete, material poverty. He means blessed are those who are not concerned with what they shall wear, or what they shall eat, or what they shall put on. He means blessed are those who have made a clear-cut choice in life and that choice is to serve one master, not two. And that master is God, not money.

Poverty of spirit and material poverty; the two go together like body and soul. You cannot have one without the other. This is the hard doctrine of Christ and few there are today who seem willing to accept it. This is hardly surprising, for even the apostles at the time of Christ found this doctrine particularly hard to take. Proof: read the story of the rich young man in St. Mark.

A rich young man kneels at the feet of Christ and says: "Good Master, what shall I do to gain eternal life?" Christ replies that he can begin by keeping the Commandments. The rich young man does keep the Commandments; as a matter of fact, he has kept them even from his youth.

In that case then: "Sell what you have and give to the poor and you will have treasure in heaven and come follow me."

Wow. This was a little more than the rich young man had bargained for. He had hoped for, perhaps, something vague and obscure, something like poverty of spirit, for example. But this took his breath away. He loved God and he kept the Commandments and maybe he even had poverty of spirit. But at the same time he had much wealth. At Christ's hard and cold suggestion that he get rid of this wealth by giving it to the poor, his face grew sad and the rich young man walked silently away.

Christ turns to his disciples who had witnessed the scene, reads their thoughts, and says: "How difficult it will be for those who have wealth to enter the kingdom of heaven. . . . It is easier for a camel to pass through the eye of a needle than for a rich man to enter the kingdom of heaven."

And St. Mark writes: "At these words the Apostles were stupefied."

Man is a creature composed of two elements: body and soul,

matter and spirit. To treat man as a disembodied spirit or as a soulless body would be absurd. It would be equally absurd to accept Christ's teaching on poverty of spirit without accepting at the same time His teaching concerning material poverty. It is a bit foolish to speak of poverty of spirit while one is living in the lap of luxury and while one is surrounded by material comfort and ease. It is equally false to speak of material poverty when one has nothing, but at the same time is eating his heart out with avarice and desire for wealth and riches.

There is a close parallel between faith and works as set down in the writings of St. Paul and St. James respectively, and material and spiritual poverty as described in St. Matthew and St. Luke. In his epistle to the Romans, St. Paul says, or at least seems to say, that man is justified by faith alone. St. James clarifies the issue by stating formally and dogmatically that faith without works is dead. In a similar way, St. Matthew seems to say that poverty of spirit is enough. St. Luke, however, shows how poverty of spirit is incomplete unless accompanied by material poverty.

Faith, like poverty of spirit, is an intellectual attitude, a spiritual adhesion, an inner conviction, and of itself and by itself it is not enough. In the second chapter of his epistle, St. James writes, "And if a brother or sister be naked and want daily food: And one of you say to them: Go in peace, be you warmed and filled; yet give them not those things that are necessary for the body, what shall it profit? So faith also, if it have not works, is dead in itself." And further in the same letter St. James writes, "Faith without works is sterile." The same may be said of poverty of spirit without the real thing: it, too, is dead and sterile.

Christianity is the religion of the Incarnation. As such, it always deals with man, not as an abstraction or a disembodied soul, but as a concrete, flesh-and-blood reality. Nothing is more realistic nor has a surer ring of inner truth than the Gospels and epistles. It is marvelous to see how St. Paul says in Romans, "I believe," and St. James follows this by saying,

"Prove it." In the same vein, St. Matthew says, "I am poor," and St. Luke seems to counter by saying, "Prove it."

One of the most solid maxims of Thomistic philosophy is: *Agere sequitur esse*, "Doing follows being." This truth is at the heart of the present discussion concerning faith and works and spiritual and material poverty. In other words, what one *is* determines what one *does*.

Someone who pretends to be poor in spirit yet gives no evidence of this in reality may be compared to someone who is intensely fond of drink yet who insists that it has no hold on him. Those who know the person suspect that he is already in the first stages of alcoholism; yet the person maintains that he is free, detached, and independent from it. "I can take it or leave it," he says, and he says it so often that he finally convinces himself that it is true. At all times, however, there is a bottle on this person's shelf and at various times of the day and night he is drawn to the bottle, like iron filings to a magnet. If the person were truly free and independent from drink, if he really could leave it, then there should be some evidence of this in his life. He must be able to prove it by giving up alcohol completely, by doing without it for a long period of time, or by reducing the portion of intake to a negligible quantity. Otherwise, the person leaves himself open to a charge of hypocrisy.

Money, wealth, comfort, and luxury can exert as strong a hold on a given individual as drink on an alcoholic. A person pretends to be free, detached, and independent from these things; he is poor in spirit, he is indifferent to them, he can take them or leave them. Yet it is a moral drama for this person to give a really generous donation to the poor. If the person's wealth is threatened he panics, and if the comfort and luxury to which this person is addicted are removed for even a short period of time the person is intensely irritable and most unhappy. The first step in the rehabilitation of an alcoholic is to persuade the alcoholic to accept himself as such. It is similar with someone addicted to money and inordinately attached to worldly possessions. If he recognizes the fact, and if he is willing to admit that he has the disease, then there is hope. If not, dry rot has already set in and there is little one can do to change the situation.

Christian poverty, if it is to be the real thing and not just a stunted cripple, must stand on two legs, one spiritual and the other material. This has been the theme of the last few pages and in support of it we have seen arguments from charity and faith. Not only charity and faith but justice as well, if applied strictly, logically, and with a Christian flair, will lead one to live, if not actually poor, at least considerably poorer than before.

In the light of justice, not only do the dispossessed and disinherited of the earth have a right to stand at the gate with outstretched hand and downcast eye to beg for the crumbs which fall from our overladen tables, but what is far more: they also have a right—God-given, innate, and inherent—to share in the food which is on the table. Why? Simply because there is enough for all and because the right to live is more basic and fundamental than the right to possess. And the right to life supersedes the right to private property.

God has created all men equal in the sense that he has given them equal dignity and equal destiny. Man's dignity is that he has been created in the image and likeness of God. His destiny, in the supernatural order, is eternal life with God. And in the natural order, it is the perfection of his natural talents, capacities, and potentialities.

This dignity and destiny, which are the heritage of every man, carry with them certain rights. Among the most basic of these are the right to food, clothing, shelter, and, later on, the right to work, and the right to marry. These rights are innate and God-given. As such, they form part of the natural law and can be neither ignored, denied, nor violated.

God, who is the author of these rights and who has created all men equal, has also created all the goods of the world for the use of all men. Not for just a few. Yet, if we were to compress the world's three and a half billion souls into one town consisting of only a thousand people, the sixty Americans in the town would receive half the income. The remaining 940 people in the town would receive the other half.

God has created a world rich enough to nourish all who cling to her for subsistence; yet, according to figures recently released by the F.A.O., two billion people are inadequately fed, clothed, and housed.

According to this same F.A.O. report, each day between 7000 and 9000 people die of causes directly attributable to malnutrition. Yet for the first time in history not only do we have enough food to feed all the people in the world, but what is equally important, we have the means to transport it. We have the planes, the steamships, the railways, the trucks and the know-how. We have the efficiency experts, the administrative geniuses, and the organization brains. We have all this and more, and yet of the thirty-five or forty million people in the world who die each year (according to a recent *Osservatore Romano*), approximately twenty million die as at least an indirect result of hunger.

We accept easily, it would seem, the logic behind the moral principle which states that if my neighbor is starving and I have bread, I must share it with him. Moreover, what I give is given in justice, not in charity. And if I do not care to give he can come and take it and his action would in no way constitute the moral evil of theft. This is quite clear.

Yet somehow the same logic becomes blurred and distorted when we attempt to project it on an international screen. Basically, the facts are just as simple.

A hundred years ago my neighbor was he who lived in the same city or town as I. Fifty years ago, with the inroads of modern transportation, my neighbor became he who lived in the same country or nation as myself. Today, in this second half of the twentieth century with no point on earth being more than twenty-four hours removed from any other point, the word "neighbor" has come to include everyone who dwells on the same planet as myself.

At present, my neighbor in South America, Asia, and Africa is hungry. He has a right then to ask for some of the bread which is on my table, and I have a corresponding obligation to share it with him. This obligation arises not from charity, but from justice.

All of which brings us back to my point of departure. Given the present world situation, and the principles of Christian charity, faith, and justice, if I have poverty of spirit, and am neither a liar nor a hypocrite, then inevitably I will be driven to embrace a life of material poverty as well.

CHAPTER NINETEEN

I N ALL THE pages of the Gospel, more space is devoted to
Christ's condemnation of hypocrisy than to any other evil.
Running a close second to hypocrisy is the evil of material
riches. Christ excoriates the two more than anything else and
his choice of language in so doing is particularly strong and
vehement.

Hypocrisy means simply to hide one's true self behind a
mask of self-righteousness, to play the phony, to kid the
world and to kid oneself into thinking that one is something
which in reality he is not. The figure of the Pharisee emerges
from the pages of the New Testament as the personification
of this sin and even to this day serves as the classic example
of hypocrisy.

The Pharisee deceived the world and himself about many
things, but most seriously about the matter of religion. He
did not realize that love is the very heart of religion, nor did
he realize that love of God and love of neighbor are not two
different values but merely two aspects of one and the same
reality. Instead, the Pharisee confused religion with things
external such as the performance of multiple rituals and the
rigid observance of a thousand and one difficult prescriptions
of the Law.

At the time of Christ, the Pharisees counted no more than
5000 or 6000 Jews in their ranks and it was only this select
handful who were really capable of performing the almost
acrobatic ritual feats demanded by their interpretation of the
Law. In so doing, the Pharisee felt that he was achieving his

own salvation before God and men and that with his own two hands he was justifying himself for time and eternity. The Pharisee lived in an ivory tower, separated from the rest of men by the complacent knowledge that he was a vastly superior creature.

Since the Gentiles and the majority of the Jews contracted legal impurity through one or another infringement of the Law, the Pharisee avoided contact with these in order to remain uncontaminated. He eventually withdrew from the human race into a holier-than-thou fortress of pious self-righteousness. The Pharisee did not like what Christ had to say about religion and he did not accept what St. John was to write later in his epistle: "He who pretends to love God Whom he does not see, and at the same time does not love his brother whom he does see, that person is a liar."

The Pharisee fought for the first place in the synagogue, liked to adorn his garments with fringe and phylacteries, and on occasion would walk boldly to the front of the temple to proclaim in a loud voice his gratitude that he was not a sinner like the rest of mankind. He did little, however, to alleviate the suffering of his fellow man and refused to be moved by the revelation of Christ as expressed in the words of St. James: "Religion pure and undefiled before God consists in helping orphans and widows in their distress."

The poverty at the time of Christ was nothing short of appalling; yet the Pharisee scrupulously avoided contact with the poor in order to avoid being legally contaminated by him. He was indifferent to this hard, cold doctrine of the Messiah as recorded by St. John: "If anyone of you, having the goods of this world and seeing his brother in need closes his heart to him, how can you say the love of God is in you?"

Isaias writes beautifully how the eternal God is singularly unimpressed by complicated fastings from food and by external penances involving sackcloth and ashes. Instead, writes the prophet, God is greatly pleased by penance and fasting which consists in the following: "Share thy bread with the hungry, give the poor and the vagrant a welcome to thy house; meet thou the naked and clothe him." The Pharisee, on the other hand, neglected his fellow man and preferred to expiate his sins before God by multiplied fastings and gaudy penances in sackcloth and ashes.

The Pharisee seems to have had little idea of what Christ was talking about when he said: "The second commandment is like unto the first, thou shalt love thy neighbor as thyself." There was such a gap between his neighbor and the Pharisee that real effective love between them was, if not impossible, at least markedly difficult.

These are a few of the reasons why Christ had so little patience with Pharisees in particular and hypocrites in general, and why he called them "whited sepulchers full of dead men's bones, clean on the outside but full of rapine and wickedness within." Christ did not abandon them, but suggested a simple practical plan of salvation which, if followed, should make them clean on the inside. "And the Lord said: Now you Pharisees make clean the outside of the cup and the platter, but your inside is full of rapine and iniquity. You fools, did not he that made that which is without, make also that which is within? But yet that which remains, give alms; and behold all things are clean unto you" (Luke 11:29–41).

The Pharisees, as we know, did not accept Christ's plan for becoming clean on the inside, and instead of giving money to the poor they continued to perform their ablutions, to stay at home on the Sabbath, and to wear their tassels to the market places. They liked this sort of activity better and it was far less painful than separating themselves from their possessions.

If Christ had little patience with hypocrites, he certainly did not have much more with those attached to material riches. Running through the pages of the New Testament almost as a leitmotiv are hard-hitting sentences such as: "It is easier for a camel to pass through the eye of a needle than for a rich man to enter the kingdom of heaven," "Woe to you who are rich for you have already had your reward," and "No man can serve two masters. You cannot serve both God and money."

Not only by words did Christ preach against riches, but his life itself is a stinging rebuke to the moneyed people of the world. Born in a stable, of poor parents, the "son" of a carpenter from an insignificant village, a wanderer, dependent on others for his food, condemned and executed as a common criminal—the historic Christ is unquestionably a Christ of poverty.

The prophet Zacharias describes the Redeemer who was to come as being both a king and a poor man, a strange contrast which Christ graphically fulfilled in his own person. Shortly before his death, Christ entered Jerusalem exactly in the manner described by the prophet, "Behold thy king who comes to thee poor, and seated upon an ass." Christ did not choose to enter Jerusalem in pomp and glory as other kings; instead he came as a poor man seated upon the lowliest of animals.

One of the finest and purest currents of religious thought running through the Old Testament is that of the *Anawin*, or "poor just man"; that is, he who submits to the oppression, suffering, and poverty of life without revolt or bitterness. Christ is the "poor just man" of the Old Testament par excellence, and it is with this in mind that Christ points to himself and proclaims, "Learn of me for I am poor and humble of heart." His public activity and method of apostolate also stand out as a forceful reproach to those attached to wealth and all that wealth represents. Christ went primarily to the poor and treated them as a privileged group. What is more, he chose his apostles and first disciples from among them. To such an extent is this true that it may be said that Christianity is the only movement in antiquity which began, grew, and spread almost uniquely through the masses of the poor.

At the very beginning of his public ministry, the Spirit of God descended upon Christ at the River Jordan and led him forth into the desert where there was only burning sand and calcified rock, solitude and monotony, union with God, and conflict with the Tempter. In the desert the Spirit of God confronted the spirit of the world, which took the form of three temptations—worldly glory, sensual pleasure, and material riches. In rejecting these temptations, the Spirit of Christ reveals himself to us, not only as a Spirit of truth and charity but a Spirit of poverty as well.

To a greater or lesser degree, the saints, too, were all driven and possessed by the same Spirit which descended upon Christ at the River Jordan. It is this Spirit who led John the Baptist into the barren wastes of Judea where his only food was locusts and wild honey, and where his only garment was a camel skin. It is this Spirit who inspired St. Paul to write, "Those things which I formerly valued I now count as loss for Christ," and "I am crucified to the world and the world to me," and again, ". . . as having nothing yet possessing all things." It is this Spirit who urged St. Francis of Assisi to espouse with such fervor his beloved "Donna Povertà," who drove John of the Cross to relentless pursuit of his "nada," and who led Charles de Foucauld further and further into the depths of "abnegation totale."

The saints have a definite role in the Church and a special function in society. They have been inspired and raised up by the Spirit of God to bring home to their contemporary fellow men in a graphic, personal, and vital way the eternal revelation of Christ. Yet we see that all the saints, in varying degree and intensity, lived lives of real material poverty and in so doing they make dramatically clear the mind of Christ on this point.

St. Francis, the Poverello of Assisi, more than any other saint perhaps, is a classic case study. In a dream or a vision Francis realized that his mission in life was to be the rebuilding of the then-crumbling Church of Jesus Christ. This much was clear. How this rebuilding was to take place, however, remained something of a mystery for Francis until one day, upon reading the Gospel of the day, he came upon the words: "And he sent them two by two . . . and he said to them: carry neither purse, nor scrip, nor shoes. . . ."

He had read these words before but never with much meaning. Now they suddenly came alive and struck home with the impact of personal discovery. Here was the answer, the secret, the way. The way was poverty.

In other words, St. Francis understood that the poverty of Christ was to be the cornerstone upon which the Church of Christ was to be strengthened and reconstructed. One pope called St. Francis the "most perfect copy of Jesus Christ," and it is interesting to note that this "most perfect copy of Jesus Christ" is also a most perfect personification of poverty, both material and the other kind.

Hypocrisy and material riches represent the antithesis of all that Christ lived, taught, and stood for. They stand at opposite poles of every value contained in the Christian *kerygma*. If this is so, one cannot help but wonder what will be the judgment of Christ, the Eternal Poorman, on a civilization which calls itself Christian and which each year spends forty-two billion dollars on entertainment, twelve billion dollars on alcohol, four billion dollars on toys for its children, two billion dollars on food for its pets, and fifty million dollars for reducing pills. And this in a world where less than twenty-four hours away thousands of people die daily of starvation.

In the time of Pope St. Gregory the Great, a beggar was reported to have died of starvation in the streets of Rome. When St. Gregory heard this, he was profoundly shocked and immediately began a complete fast which lasted three days and three nights. Today, in places less than twenty-four hours removed, at least 7000 people die daily of hunger, yet who in America would dream of missing a meal for them, or a dessert, or, for that matter, even a cigarette?

As long as there is one person in the world who is hungry, Christ also is hungry. As long as there is one person in the world who is sick, Christ suffers in him. As long as there is one person who is cold and ill clothed, Christ is also. This is not poetry but solid Catholic dogma. Yet there are hundreds of millions of such people in the world today. The only way one can manifest solidarity with them and with Christ in them, the only way one can become really clean on the inside, is to tighten one's belt, sacrifice, and really give. This in no way should be regarded as something unusual or heroic. It is a simple directive which in one form or another is found on every page of the New Testament and which ultimately separates the followers of Christ from the followers of the Pharisees.

♦

CHAPTER TWENTY

♦

WHILE IN EUROPE, I took Bishop Choi on pilgrimage to a favorite haunt of mine. The name of the place is Banneux, and it is located in the Ardennes Mountain region of eastern Belgium.

It was Bishop Choi's first meeting with the Virgin of the Poor and he went away profoundly impressed. As for myself it was perhaps the twelfth time I had been to Banneux. As a seminarian I went often to ponder the mystery of the Mother of God who appears to a poor child of Belgium and leaves her a message of hope for the poor and little ones not only of Belgium but of the whole world.

The story is brief and soon told.

The year is 1933, the day is January 15, the time—7:30 P.M. Mariette Beco, eleven years of age, eldest of a family of eleven children, daughter of a poor laborer, rustic, forthright, not especially inclined to piety, is looking out the window of her house when she sees a light. After her eyes adjust to the light she makes out the form of a beautiful Lady, clothed in white garments and wearing a cincture of blue. The Lady beckons the child to come out, her parents forbid her, the child looks again, the light and the Lady are gone; thus ends the first apparition.

The Mother of God is not known for being especially loquacious. So it is when she appears to the children of men her words are few and far between, but they are chosen with care. At Banneux, for example, in a total of eight apparitions

Our Lady speaks no more than a dozen sentences, all of which are short, simple, and marvelously profound.

First Apparition: silence.

Second Apparition: "Put your hands into the water. This spring is reserved for me. Bon soir, au revoir."

Third Apparition: "I am the Virgin of the Poor. This spring is reserved for all nations to comfort the sick. I will pray for you. Au revoir."

Fourth Apparition: "I would like to have a small chapel."

Fifth Apparition: "I come to relieve suffering. Au revoir."

Sixth Apparition: "Believe in me, I will believe in you. Pray very much. Au revoir."

Seventh Apparition: "My dear child, pray very much. Au revoir."

Eighth Apparition: "I am the Mother of the Saviour, Mother of God. Pray very much. Adieu."

That's all there is, yet it was enough to give a number of theologians and bishops many a headache as they struggled to unravel its meaning. Ecclesiastical approval was slow in coming—in all it took more than fifteen years—but when it finally did come it was complete and enthusiastic.

At Lourdes, Our Lady, with that fine flair for dramatic simplicity which characterizes her, said: "I am the Immaculate Conception." Seventy-five years later at Banneux Our Lady says: "I am the Virgin of the Poor," and this title shines forth as the gem of the apparitions.

In choosing such a title and applying it to herself, Our Lady reveals herself as being unmistakably and compassionately class-conscious. This is hardly surprising, for after all she is the Mother of a Son who more than 2000 years ago identified himself with the class of the poor. Beginning with Guadalupe, continuing through La Salette, Lourdes, Fatima, Beauraing, and right down to Banneux, Our Lady chose her favorites from among the very poor in much the same manner as Christ chose his Apostles from among this same class.

At Banneux we are reminded of an oft-neglected, yet

rather important, fact of Christianity. It is this: in the City of God poverty is a status symbol which separates the "ins" from the "outs."

A few weeks after visiting Banneux, Bishop Choi and I went on another pilgrimage—this time to Lourdes. At Lourdes we were reminded of another important fact, namely that the world is sick.

Mary, the Mother of God, made a statement similar to this a hundred years ago—and she repeated it at Fatima sixty years later. In effect she said: "The world is sick. . . . People must pray and do penance or else the world will perish." And this sick world of which Mary speaks is primarily the Western world, the Christian world, to wit: Europe and America.

Who would believe it? Who would believe that this so proud Western civilization of ours is afflicted with a sickness, a serious one at that, judging from the tone of voice and the choice of words used by the Mother of God.

Our workmen put in fewer hours and draw fatter paychecks than ever before. Our farmers, with much less toil and on smaller plots of ground, produce far richer yields than any other farmers in history. Our scientists split the atom, explore the stars, tap the ocean depths, invent machines that think and machines that talk. Our doctors eradicate disease, eliminate pain, and keep our citizens alive longer than the citizens of any other civilization in the world. And yet there is a sickness?

It is not just talk. There are signs of this sickness and there are indications that all is not right with the world. One of the most striking of these signs is the fantastically lopsided distribution of the material wealth of the world. It is a sign which hits one like a blow in the face, unless perhaps one protects his head by burying it in the sand. The picture of a fat, rich, opulent Western society in a lean, hungry, and starving world is clear indication that somewhere deep inside there is a very serious spiritual disturbance.

In America people work eight hours a day in air-conditioned

offices, come home to meals of steak and apple pie, watch TV at night, and in the summer climb into expensive cars to motor to the seashore and mountains. The principal preoccupations of American society are relaxation and enjoyment. One of the principal fears is obesity. This society has been referred to on various occasions as: "the affluent society," "the leisure society," "the cosmetic society," "the pleasure society," even "the aphrodisiac society." It has been written that the people of this culture measure their life out in coffee spoons and that the monument to their generation will be a thousand lost golf balls.

In Korea, in all of Asia, in Africa, and in South America things are a little different. For the vast majority of people living in these areas, happiness is a full bowl of rice at mealtime and a warm roof over one's head at bedtime. The principal preoccupation of these people is: Where does the next meal come from? And their principal fear is: What happens when I get sick? The society in these lands is called "the have-not society" and the future monument to its members will be a thousand empty rice bowls.

In terms of miles and distance there is not much that separates the have-not society from the affluent society. As a matter of fact, the two societies are less than a day apart. In terms of bread and butter, however, there is a chasm between the two worlds and more than a thousand light-years between the shores.

Christ came to earth and walked and spoke and taught, not as a philosopher or a theologian, but as a man of the people. He spoke the language of the people and the people understood him. Yet he always remained a mystic and a poet. When he looked at the world about him, for example, he did not see what other men saw. He saw a more profound, hidden spiritual reality. When he saw the sky growing red and threatening a storm he thought of the last judgment. When on the road to Jerusalem he came upon a withered fig tree, he was reminded of the spiritual barrenness of the

Jewish people. When his gaze rested upon a field of golden wheat swaying in the breeze he thought of the multitude of souls in the world ripe for the spiritual harvest but in desperate need of priests and apostles.

If Christ, the poet and the mystic, were to look about the world today and see the overwhelmingly unjust distribution of wealth in the world, he would say exactly what his mother said for him at Lourdes and Fatima: "The world is sick." He would look upon all this as an irrefutable sign that men do not love each other, that they do not love enough to sacrifice for each other, that they do not love each other as Christ has loved them. And he would probably say again what he said 2000 years ago and what Mary repeated at Lourdes: "Unless you do penance you shall perish." When he spoke of penance he had in mind primarily the type of penance that Isaiah referred to: Break bread to the hungry, clothe the naked, and welcome the stranger.

Each year in America, in the spring, summer, and fall, expensive tours are organized to places of pilgrimage such as Lourdes and Fatima. Any Catholic with sufficient funds is welcome to go along. He will most likely stay in a hotel, wine and dine in an enjoyable manner, journey comfortably to the scene of the apparitions, and be piously moved by stirring sermons and impressive processions. When he returns home, the pilgrim will probably feel that he got his thousand dollars' worth.

But, I wonder, did he get the message? Did the message that the world is sick, really sick, hit him hard and shake him up so that he is very disturbed about it? Did the message that he must do penance—not the "don't eat meat on Friday" type of penance, but the "sell what you have and give to the poor" type of penance—did this message strike home?

I have thought of a scheme which I shall try one day. Just for laughs. The idea is this: I will slip a bribe to the pilot of one of those big shiny Lourdes-bound pilgrimage planes, and after takeoff the pilot will turn the plane in the direction of Korea instead of France. He will bring the plane down in Pusan, and I will be at the airport to meet the pilgrims.

After welcoming them I will lead them in procession into Pusan. I will take them through the squalid streets of this city of slums, pointing out to them on my right and on my left the hovels of the poor, the squatter huts of the refugees, the lean-to's in which the ragpickers dwell, the barracks which house the TB patients. They would see the beggars, the orphan boys in the streets, the people waiting in front of feeding stations for cornmeal and flour. Finally I would take the pilgrims to the city dump, why not? Our Lady first announced to Bernadette that the world was sick at what was then the city dump of Lourdes! I would take them here and let them see for themselves a most unpretty sight: women and children with blackened and scarred hands scraping in the refuse for morsels of food to eat and bits of junk to sell.

Then I would lead them back to the plane (there is really no place in Pusan where they could be comfortably lodged). After the people were comfortably seated and the plane was ready to take off, I would simply repeat what Our Lady said at Lourdes: "The world is sick."

Ten to one they would believe me.

REV. ALOYSIUS SCHWARTZ
P. O. BOX 60
PUSAN, KOREA

DATE DUE

GAYLORD			PRINTED IN U.S.A.